A LITTLE BOOK ON RELIGION
(for people who are not religious)

OTHER BOOKS BY SAMUEL SANDMEL

A Jewish Understanding of the New Testament
(1956, Ktav)

Philo's Place in Judaism
(1956, Hebrew Union College Press; 1971, Ktav)

The Genius of Paul
(1959, Farrar, Straus and Company; 1971, Schocken)

The Hebrew Scriptures: An Introduction to Their Literature and Religious Ideas
(1963, 1968, Knopf)

We Jews and Jesus
(1965, Oxford)

Herod: Profile of a Tyrant
(1967, Lippincott)

We Jews and You Christians: An Inquiry into Attitudes
(1967, Lippincott)

The First Christian Century in Judaism and Christianity
(1969, Oxford)

The Several Israels
(1971, Ktav)

Two Living Traditions: Essays in Bible and Religion
(1972, Wayne State University Press) (The Jewish Book Council Award for 1972)

Old Testament Issues, Editor
(1968, Harper & Row)

The Enjoyment of Scripture
(1972, Oxford)

Alone Atop the Mountain (a novel about Moses)
(1973, Doubleday)

Ecumenical Introductions to the Books of the Bible, Co-author
(1974, The Catholic Press)

Judaism and Christian Beginnings
(Oxford) in preparation

A LITTLE BOOK ON RELIGION

(for people who are not religious)

SAMUEL SANDMEL

WILSON BOOKS

To

my Class of Townspeople

who have made the hours together

so gratifying to a teacher

WILSON BOOKS are published for the Liberal Arts by
Conococheague Associates, Inc.
1053 Wilson Avenue
Chambersburg, Pennsylvania 17201.

Library of Congress Catalog Card Number: 75-1831
International Standard Book Number: 0-89012-002-1

This book is for the neglected, for parents or grandparents who either have no religious roots or have forgotten or abandoned whatever roots they had.

Certainly a concern for the young is important. But their elders too have the right to a fullness of life.

TABLE OF CONTENTS

CHAPTER

Preface

MOST OF WHAT I have written has come from the classroom, writing that has been directly or indirectly related to facets of scholarship. Not this book. It comes from the living room, where I have been someone's guest, or from my own living room where people — cultured, intelligent, but with no academic or scholarly interest, or background — have been my guests. How often have these intelligent and earnest people turned the conversation to religion! How often have they seemed confused or thoroughly misinformed!

How strange sometimes are the views and ideas that exist! How little factual information about religion do even cultured people possess, and how fuzzy is the knowledge about religious ideas.

Part of the difficulty is the tone of our age. Usual terms for it are "secular," or "naturalistic," and religion, so it is inferred, is out of keeping with it. Also, many a thoughtful person has been taught about religion only when a child, and a young child at that, and makes a ready equation between this childish religion and the religion of mature people. Even among nominally religious people, affiliation is often more a matter of form — the social thing to do — than of conviction, and, indeed, some such people seem at times to have a sense of shame about the affiliation, justifying it as for the sake of children. Such ambivalence is often, so it seems to me, the product of some single college course, either in the "philosophy of religion," or else in Bible. I have observed reflections of the philosophy of religion in this way, that an apparently admirable, well-taught course, accepted certain premises about basic information, but began at a level beyond the basic information, with the consequence that I have had the impression that the person understood the philosophy part of philosophy of religion, but not the religion part. Or else someone has had a course in Bible and learned and remembers facets of the modern scholarship on the Bible, but seems to have failed to penetrate beyond the scholarship into the Bible itself.

This little book is by design a book of explanation, to tell mature people without religion what religion is about. It is an argument on behalf of religion in only one sense, namely, the supposition that mature understanding can possibly help some people remove those unnecessary obstacles which bar them from religion or religion from them. In manner, the book is, so I hope, neither preachy nor exhortative. I have preferred to treat matters briefly so that, in short compass, I may be able to show the breadth of concerns in religion. I hope I have not sacrificed responsible exposition by writing briefly.

Because of the nature of the audience for whom I am writing, I have shunned both the jargon of theologians and even the word *theology*. This latter word underwent some scorn in the nineteenth century (as is true of the word *theologize* even today). To secular-minded university professors, theology signified the worst aspect of all the heritage of religion; "philosophy of religion" became a kind of acceptable substitute in colleges for the unacceptable word theology.

Now theology is, or ought to be, an orderly, systematic inquiry into the phenomena of a Religion, bearing a relationship, as some have put it, like that of botany to the flowers, plants, and trees. In the middle ages, theology was known as the "queen of the sciences," and philosophy was its handmaiden. The scorn or suspicion of theology arose from misuse and abuse, for there were those who tried to force their views onto others and to deprive the inquiring mind of the freedom to question and to express opinions. Again, there were those who tended to trivialize the whole enterprise by a preoccupation with remote or irrelevant or speculative abstractions, these satirized in the question "How many angels can dance on the point of a pin?"

There is still a residual scorn of theology. One aspect of it is capable of irking me, namely, the ordinary practice among many Christians and some Jews to term special topics the "theology" of this or that; for example, the legitimate concern about the necessary attention a local church needs to give its fiscal affairs hardly justifies calling this concern a "theology of church administration." Useful probings scarcely need such grandiloquent nomenclature as, "a theology of Christian-Jewish relations," "a theology of women's liberation," or "black theology." The word *theology*, one notes sorrowfully, is all too often part of shallow clerical rhetoric.

These comments are meant as a prelude to a very important conclusion. While not everything labeled theology merits that accolade, when theology is truly a reasoned, profound inquiry into man and God and the nature of religion, it is to my mind the most important of all human inquiries and academic disciplines.

While in a sense this is a book of theology, the effort here does not merit so lofty an acclaim. Rather, my effort is both modest and restricted (and genuine theology beyond my capacities and disposition). This little book is essentially only explanation, and not more than that.

I frequently define the sense of a term as I use it. Dictionaries are usually aimed at a general audience, with the result that a succinct definition can be accurate without being clear. Moreover, words have overtones, and these I try to give, simply because a usual dictionary does not.

I have deliberately confined my attention to western man and religion in the West. About the eastern religions, which I deeply respect, my opinion is that only after one understands that which is near at hand is one qualified to go to what is distant. By all means, let a person deepen himself by learning about these religions. But for a person to espouse an eastern religion prior to achieving a good understanding of what is in his immediate environment seems to me to lead to falling short of truly grasping the eastern. An eastern cultural expression, like Zen Buddhism, or Indian religions, can for many westerners be a mere fad which debases a worthy religion.

I keep stressing a "little book." It could easily have been more extended — I have written books much longer. I have deliberately tried to be brief, fully aware that I have dealt in a paragraph with what could have consumed a book, as is the case throughout what I have here chosen to include. I have not tried to tell all I know, but only to select what I have thought a reader should have some knowledge of. I am reasonably satisfied in this regard, though aware of deliberate omissions and of having compressed complexities into some recurrently general statements.

In a different regard, I am not pleased: The matters dealt with are intertwined; at times, in dealing with one topic, I have felt the need to introduce aspects of others, though these are dealt with elsewhere in the book. There is, hence, some inevitable need for cross-reference; to help the reader, I have deemed it wise to indulge in some repetitions.

I

Religion and the Religions

RELIGION IS THE thought and feeling that a person has about aspects of living which are greater and deeper than the person himself, and in essence beyond him. It seeks for answers to questions such as these: What is the relationship in time between the now and here where I exist and what has preceded me and also is to come after me? What is the relationship of my own circle of geographical experience and acquaintance to the boundless geography and space beyond me? How am I personally related to all this?

Religion seeks for answers to these questions, and often supplies them. Sometimes what it finds can persuade one person and not another, but the point is that religion proceeds beyond the asking of questions into the effort to answer them.

Why do people ask questions about the relationship of the here and now to what is beyond them? One reason is the natural curiosity among human beings. Inevitably, we humans encounter events or situations which appeal to us as effects of antecedent causes, and it is the way of human beings to try to answer the important question: "What caused this?" We ask this sort of question in such humdrum things as the failure of our car or television set to work properly; it is usual, when we come to the repairman, to ask him: "What caused this?"

In a dimension quite beyond mere curiosity, we — we ourselves, or our representatives — ask this question about cause in cases of military involvements or disasters, or in tragedies such as the crash of an airplane. At such times our purpose may be to

1

affix blame; at other times it is to learn from the one particular accident how other such accidents can be averted.

There is often, however, a different kind of curiosity which in some given situation is an urgent necessity to a person. For example, suppose I invested my life's savings in a gilt-edge stock, and by some strange development the stock were to lose most or all of its value so that I was wiped out financially. It would be natural for me to want to know how this could have happened, and happened to me. In fact, my wish to learn what had happened could be urgent, or even desperate, for conceivably I would never know inner peace of mind unless I could find some gratifying answer.

The primary "why" questions in religion — not the only ones, to be sure, but surely the primary ones — have to do with living and not living, that is, of being born, of growing — coming to physical maturity, marrying and begetting — and of dying. These "milestone" events ordinarily appear to intrude upon us, for they interrupt our ordinary and unthinking routines, since normally we give little direct thought or attention to these matters. Thus, when a child is born to us, we are often moved, especially in the case of a first child, to contemplate the wonder of it. That that child was conceived in the act of sexual intercourse is not usually a sufficient or appropriate answer, for, as we marvel at a baby's fingers and toes and tiny mouth, and its ability to cry and soon thereafter to laugh, we begin to ask ourselves, how did this tiny baby come to be alive, and just what is living that this little baby participates in, and how did such living originate? Comparably, when there is a death near to us, or when the knowledge we all so soon acquire that some day we too will die, comes to us, we can wonder how life began that it must end. At puberty and marriage too, in less intense ways, such questions may also occur. The data which we can learn from medicine and biology, correct as it may be, may satisfy us but only partially, for the answer that we seek involves something more basic than mere biology.

We do not all ask these questions with the same fervor, or

2

always with the same eagerness or anxiety; indeed, some of us are able to ask such questions without ever framing them in spoken or unspoken words; we may have within us only a vague sense of questioning. Yet such questions, whether asked openly or only vaguely pondered, are a reality in the experience of all people who live at least into the teens, for these perennial questions are universal.

Because these questions look for the ultimate answers (in the dimension of asking, What is life?), not the proximate answers (that a baby comes out of sexual intercourse), the frequent elusiveness of ready or satisfying answers suggests that the profound answers lie far below the surface of routine living. All of us, in some way or other, make a distinction between appearance, between how things seem to be, and an underlying reality which is not visible on the surface. Such a distinction between appearance and something which is deeper is very ancient; it has reappeared in various forms at various intervals in past history. In our own time, if we meet a cruel, vindictive person, we begin to ask ourselves what motivates that person, and we often indulge in speculation about that person's psyche, or what childhood experiences made him what he is. Or else, in our complicated economic world, we can notice that prices rise or fall, and we quickly attribute these to good or poor production, but thereupon some commentator on TV or in the press emerges to assure us that latent forces, quite removed from good or poor production, are the true explanation.

Religion has to do both with the visible and the tangible and also with a possible underlying reality not present on the surface.

Because we human beings both think and also feel, we respond to appearance and the underlying reality both with our minds and with our hearts. With our minds, we reason as best we can, normally trying to move back from an effect to its specific cause. With our hearts we modify our reason, as with hope or despair; we engage, in the various forms of our activities, in guesses or hunches; or we can become so tenacious of some particular goal

3

or objective that we describe our desire to reach it by the term *obsession*. Often it is our hopes or anxieties which propel us into our beginning to think; without such prompting we might not persist in trying to think things through. At the same time, once we have begun our thinking, our hearts are able to impede or distort our ability to think clearly.

The milestones of our lives, yielding joy or sorrow, anticipation or fear, or anxiety or despair, are more apt to be what sets us to thinking about religion than simply the capacity that we possess to think. I should imagine — I have no statistics — that sorrow, fear, and anxiety more frequently propel us towards religious questions than do joy or exultation. There are some people who, agreeing with this judgment, proceed to find in it a basis for scorning those people who seek religious answers. I find this hard to understand, for sorrow, fear, and anxiety are human experiences, and I do not see that there is any basis to denigrate religion in those cases in which such factors have prompted it. What is more natural than that some human emotion should propel an individual into religious inquiry?

There are some people who are persuaded, in fullest honesty and integrity, that there are no valid ultimate answers to the questions which religion asks, and they conclude that they are without religion. We can grant the good faith of such people. Yet in the sense that religion deals with these kinds of questions, even that person who comes to negative and negating answers is himself within the realm of religion. We must not here be led astray into merely playing with words. I am not asserting that such people are religious; I am saying only that by the very act of denying the genuine existence of a religious dimension to life, they have crossed the border wherein the word *religion* applies.

That religion is almost universal among men does not mean that it takes the same form or has the same emphases everywhere, for manifestly this is not true. Moreover, religion is in one sense always personal, a reflection of the individual way in which a person arrays his thoughts and feelings. Necessarily this

4

varies from person to person. Such is the case even for the adherent of a particular Religion (Judaism, Christianity, or Islam). A Religion, especially a very ancient one, may have distinctive corporate practices, distinctive obligatory ideas, and a distinctive mode of organization; no matter how faithful the communicant is to all of these, he does not completely lose his individuality in the corporate entity.

Many factors have shaped an abiding ancient Religion: history, ideas, persons, and geography. We all know that our age has inherited many Religions. Some Religions arose so distantly from others as to be quite distinctive and "different"; others have been derived from older religions, as Christianity derived from Judaism, so that Judaism and Christianity present both overlap and crucial difference. For our purposes, we shall mean by a Religion with a capital "R" an entity that managed at some point in the past to achieve a certain corporate existence, and to become perpetuated through its adherents. In virtually all such Religions there are to be found answers offered to the questions which every individual is prone to ask. Indeed, in some traditions, the answers provided are conceived of as obligatory on the communicant. These inherited answers, whether obligatory or only suggestive, are often a legacy of ages long since past which arose in areas far removed from where the modern adherent may chance to reside; at times such answers are so definitely a product of so ancient a time and of so remote a place as to defy ready modern understanding; further to complicate matters, decisive changes in the outlook of men in general have raised for men of our time the problem of the tenability of the ancient answers even when they are understood. An ancient Religion confronts man with a ledger which, on the side of assets, is a record of the profound search by men for answers, and on the side of liabilities the possibility that the answers appear outmoded. Many modern men do not view ancient Religion as an affirmative heritage into which one can legitimately fit his personal religion, but rather as a strait jacket, or else a Procrustean bed, distorting or even destroying an individual's acute sense of

5

personal integrity. Such modern men are apt to regard personal religion and an ancient Religion as though they are opposites to the point of being incongruous with each other. Such men are at times pushed even further towards a needless sense of contrast or contradiction by zealous adherents, usually from among the clergy, who so misunderstand the modern temper as to believe that modern man can be compelled and coerced; the reality is that modern men can possibly be persuaded to religion or a Religion, but never coerced to it.

I shall need to assume a certain open-mindedness on the part of the reader. Such open-mindedness is urgent because there is a tendency to rigidity among all of us, with the result that we equate the childhood experience we have had with a particular Religion as normative, as if that childhood experience is the measuring rod for all else that can and should be learned about religion. How useful it would be for a reader to be able to divest himself of the practice of equating his own childhood experience with the exhaustive totality of religion! Perhaps people follow such a tendency in all facets of life, whether of patriotism or literary appreciation; in other areas, though, growth in perception and in the depth of insight seems possible. Can this be the case with religion?

Our general procedure will entail providing a threefold exposition, one, an exposition of a component element of religion; next, an illustration of the way in which that element has appeared in traditional Religions, and third — where relevant — how a modern person might understand this matter.

I am aware that for some possible readers I have written with excessive explanation; I hope that my wish for clarity has not too often resulted in laboring a point; where I have done so, it is because my experience in teaching has led me to think that some abstractions require laboring.

6

II

Knowledge and Belief

CRUCIAL IN ENSUING discussions are some distinctions (at once simple and yet, in my experience, confusing), between knowledge and belief. The use of these words in this book requires that author and reader have some good agreement on what these words are here taken to mean.

Suppose I am asked, How far is it from Cincinnati to Chicago? I could answer, "four and a half hours driving time"; or, "slightly less than an hour by plane"; or, after adding up figures on a road map, "about 300 miles." In all three cases some rather ready verification from published materials is possible. Knowledge implies a realistic possibility of verification.

Suppose, though, that I have at hand no ready means of verification. I might say, "I believe it is three hundred miles." Belief exists in the area wherein precise verification is not readily possible. If I know, I am exempt from having to believe; if I say, "I believe," the implication is that I do not actually know.

But, now to change things slightly, suppose I am asked, "When did the Civil War begin?" At the moment of asking, I have no history books or encyclopedias around, and verification is not at hand. If my memory chances to be an unusually good one, I might venture to say, "I *know* it began in 1861." If I have only a limited confidence in my memory, I might say, "I *think* it began in 1861." In this sense, think represents a certainty less than knowing but implies that the facts can be gotten. Suppose that two people begin a quarrel (as can happen in a parlor, again where history books are not hand); one person opts for 1860, and the other for 1861. If, in the course of the quarrel, each embraces his chosen date, each might say, "Not only do I *think* it began in 1860 or 1861, but I *believe* my date is the right one." To believe in this sense is something quite other than knowing, and expresses a measure of certainty (about something as yet unverified) that goes beyond mere thinking.

In a religious sense, to believe is different than to know, and it goes beyond the merely tentative character of to think. In a strict sense, wherever and whenever I can verify something, in that case I should say, "I know"; wherever I cannot verify, now or later, that is a case when I should say, "I believe." If I do not know, and have not yet arrived at a feeling of certainty, I should then say, "I think." Most people use such words loosely; in this book we must not.

Let us now abandon the matter of "I think," and concentrate on "I know" and "I believe." I shall use *know* and *believe* as opposites, for *know* will imply that data are either already at hand or are readily to be gotten, but *believe* means that I will never, never truly possess the necessary data. We must rule out here a frequent careless use of *know* where in effect it means only *believe*. A teacher who, on entering a classroom, finds an indecent sentence on the blackboard, scrutinizes all members of the class, and, from circumstantial evidence, may conclude that John Doe is the culprit; even though she cannot prove this, she is subjectively certain; she might say, "I know that John Doe did this." Challenged by a denial on the part of the student, she may be vexed to the point of saying, with emphatic certainty, "I positively know that John Doe did this." Yet, unless unmistakable verification is possible, this use (really abuse) of *know* should not disguise the reality that the teacher firmly believes, but does not truly know. We must try not to confuse such use of know and believe. In religious discussions, it is not infrequent that someone who fervently believes will say something kindred to, "I know God exists." In our discussion in the ensuing pages, though I shall speak of this inner sense of certainty, I shall, how-

8

ever, rigidly restrict *know* to what is verifiable, and *believe* to to what is not and cannot be verified.

Since knowing implies possible verification, and belief its impossibility, I shall proceed to use the terms in the sense of different extents, or degrees, and illustrate this difference in the following example. "I know that Washington was the first president of the United States"; "I believe he was the greatest of all presidents." The first statement can be verified, the second scarcely. "I know that Jesus was a Jew" is a reflection of verifiable knowledge; "I believe Jesus was the Incarnate Son of God" is a belief, not subject to the same kind of verifiable knowledge.

If I say, "Washington was the tenth president," I can be proved wrong (insofar as reasonable proof operates). Even after being proved wrong, I may continue to hold my erroneous opinion. If I do so, I am substituting an untenable belief for ascertainable fact. Many people do this, especially religious people, and they thereby become quite capricious. The view in this book is that a religious belief is untenable if it contradicts knowable facts.

But it is quite a different matter if one turns to belief after one has first exhausted the available facts. The teacher, having made the best inquiry she could, could say, "I do not know who wrote the indecent sentence on the blackboard. I am acquainted with the class; I see something striking in the handwriting. Therefore, I firmly *believe* it was John Doe." Or, one can say, "I do not *know* how the world came to exist; I have studied history, astronomy, geology, physics, and chemistry, but these studies have not given me a final answer. Now I am ready to say, 'I *believe* that the world exists because God created it.'"

Belief, in the sense of its use in this book, never contradicts what we can know. Belief is a stage we may come to when we have moved in fullest measure through all that we can know.*

*I shall treat later (chapter XX) a recurrent Christian view that has held that a Christian is justified in believing quite against contradictory knowledge.

I shall use *belief* and *faith* in quite different senses. Faith, as I shall use it, will have nothing to do with knowledge or lack of it. Rather, faith will mean reliance on God. My attitude to my mother when I was young was that of faith, that of perfect reliance on her. If, though, I spoke of her mind, or her moral character, I would mean my beliefs about her (I believe she was wise, I believe she was honorable).

To have faith in God is to have perfect reliance on him. The word faith expresses my *attitude to him*, whatever he may be. My beliefs reflect my *thoughts about him*, such as my efforts to describe him, but not directly to my attitude towards him.

To summarize, if I *know*, I need not call on my capacity to *believe*, for I believe only when I am not in a position to know. Once I have believed — about God, or about people, or about ideas — and I feel touched or moved by these, I can speak of my faith in them. Faith is my subjective feeling about my belief or beliefs; I can express my faith or let it remain unexpressed.

I should want a necessary distinction to be clear between the words *credible* and *true*. It is a fact that many people can believe what is untrue or disbelieve what is true. Yet most educated, thinking people will not believe in what is incredible, since they hold that they will believe in only what is true. Credible, however, simply means believable; my use of the word is not meant as a final judgment on whether the matter is true or not.

Much of inherited religious doctrine has become "incredible"; that is, modern men will not or cannot believe that it is true. To say this does not mean that such a doctrine is not true. Much of our discussion will need to take account of this matter of credibility and truth.

Last, it is necessary to try to distinguish between religion and superstition. The distinction is difficult, for aspects of the Religions, especially their rituals, grew out of superstition, and overtones of the latter abide in the Religions. By *superstition*, I will mean the supposition that a man has available to him resources by which to control what he believes are supernatural forces beyond him. If thirteen people are at a dinner and exposed to some hidden danger simply because thirteen is an unlucky number, I can "control" the force beyond me either by increasing or decreasing the number. In the case of other superstitions, the device of magic may seem helpful — whether it be carrying a rabbit's foot or reciting some incantation. In general, supersition is a belief, while magic is an instrument for carrying out a belief.

Religion is man's quest for understanding and adjustment to what is beyond man. Religion is not religion if it pretends to control what is beyond man.

III

The Existence of God

HOW CAN MAN learn to *know* that God exists? (This question is different from the question, What is God?) The answer is that man *cannot*. What man can do is to reach further and further back in time, through science, to answer the question, How did things (including life as we know it) come to exist? The situation, however, is still this: no matter how far back in time we can reach with geology and astronomy, we cannot reach beyond that point in time when *something* existed.

All theories of the origin of the world, the universe, and matter, regardless of what remote point they push to, deal with something that has already come to exist — however primitive such existence may appear to be, such as primitive life, or the beginnings of our solar and planetary systems. Science cannot yet explain how they came to exist. God is often used as the term for that cause out of which things have come to exist. Whatever has come to exist, whether in primitive or complicated form, is the effect of that cause. God, as it were, is the answer which arises at the point where we exhaust what is known and what can be known about the origin of what has come into being. God, then, becomes the explanation for the unknown and unknowable. God, if we believe in him, enters in at the stage when we exhaust what we can know and proceed into the unknowable. The only options available about God are to believe or not to believe, but never to know.

Not to believe in God is to be left without an explanation for the ultimate.

But to believe entails some very formidable problems.

IV

The Meaning of the Term God

NOT EVERYTHING that could and should be said about God can appear in this chapter. Certain important ideas will be touched on, but not here fully developed. Perhaps the reader might turn back to the Table of Contents to glimpse some of the other topics which will enter in later on. Here the principal purpose will be to set forth what it is that men have had in mind when they have used the word *God*. Whether we accept or reject their opinions, they all help us in clarifying our own thought and in deepening it.

To speak about God requires words. It is a truism that without words we cannot communicate, but even with them, communication can be difficult and misleading. If I were to say, for example, that God created the world, and thereafter we composed a sentence in which a pronoun would be used, what would be the pronoun? For example, suppose my sentence is this: "When God first created the world, *He* began with nothing." But should I perhaps substitute the word *It* for the word He — or the word *She*? If I speak of prayer to God, and of the conviction which people have had that prayer ascends to God, may I say: "God *hears* prayer?" Do I mean by my using the word *hears* that God has ears, like yours or mine? Manifestly, I would not mean that. Now, I cannot discuss God without using the words that ordinarily apply to human beings, like seeing or hearing, even though I may firmly believe that God does not have eyes or ears, or sees and hears, the way that human beings do. Hence, I find myself in a constant dilemma, for I must resort to words to communicate, but the words I use fall short of what is exactly meant.

In general, what people mean by God is that there is a certain Power that has been and is extant in the world, and that this Power is such that it is free of and immune to man's demonstrable weakness and transience and inevitable passing. Yet Power is not precisely the word we mean, for it implies force, such as an engine possesses, but only when it is turned on. Power should not simply imply coercion. But perhaps we might express this idea more clearly by a contrast, namely, that we mean by Power the exact opposite of the limits of power demonstrable in man. Thus, to some basic questions which we recurrently ask, the answers would never be Man. For example, we would never say that Man created the world, that Man created life, that Man governs the universe. Whether we believe that God does exist or does not exist, we can perhaps now be reasonably clear with each other when we say that the word *God*, for those who have believed in him, has been associated with exactly those capacities which man lacks. This is true, even though we have no recourse but to use human terms in talking about God.

The word *God*, thus, serves as a short-cut term to allude to matters which are the opposite of human. As a short-cut term, it can offer to some people a full and ready answer — perhaps too full and too ready an answer — to either the mystery of how everything began, or the frightening or joyously overwhelming aspects of living. Indeed, for some such people, the mere word *God* is in itself a sufficient answer, with an implication that nothing more needs to be asked.

But for most people, especially for the thoughtful, a veritable host of new questions arise. One such question is, "*What* is God?" Is he only a vague force, totally unlike man, or is he some entity residing in some particular place — such as heaven — and does he have particular characteristics, in a way similar to characteristics which men have? Whence did he originate? What does he do to occupy his time? What is his relationship to

14

men — is he in touch or out of touch with them? Does he expect something from men, such as the worship of him, or obedience to him? Do men come to the opinion that a God exists solely out of man's capacity to reason from effect back to cause (that is, the world is here and we are in it, and the world and we are a result of some antecedent cause we call God), or, instead, are there on record credible accounts of specific historic occasions on which God and man came into direct contact, even into conversation, with each other? If so, then God is not a matter that has come out of man's reasoning, but out of experiences of the race of men. Are there also on record old, inherited accounts of direct contact between God and men that today seem incredible?

V

God in the Bible

ALL OF US born into the western world inherit a legacy, including some view or views about God, from Judaism or Christianity. For only a few of us has that legacy been a matter of any depth of inquiry or of acceptance. The knowledge by most of us of Judaism and Christianity is usually superficial or even shallow and erroneous.

Now, to the question, What is God, as in the Bible?

The biblical literature does not raise the question, Is there a God? Rather, it assumes that there is one. Twice in Psalms (14:1; 53:1) allusion is made to the "fool who says in his heart there is no God." Most scholars hold that it is not the existence that the fool denies, but rather the significance, or the power of God, that he rejects.

What is common in virtually all the books of Old and New Testaments is the set of implicit beliefs that its God once created the universe and still rules it, and that he came into a set and series of relations with his people at specific times and places.

Only in a limited sense does the biblical literature actually tell what God is. That limited extent is a written record in the Bible concerning what he was purported to have done (such as creation, or his imposing laws on man). From what he is presented as having done, we might infer what he is. Hence, the following brief summary: For the Hebrews, it was he who creat the world and ruled it. Having created the earth, he gave it to the human race for its dominion. Man, too, was a creature, something created; all humanity was descended from one pair,

16

Adam and Eve, the first created humans. The inhabitants of the three continents known in ancient times had descended from Noah's three sons: the Asians from Shem, the Africans from Ham, and the people of the Greek areas from Japheth.

In Asia there had emerged God's chosen people, the Hebrews. Three solitary patriarchs, Abraham, Isaac, and Jacob, had been the first in the chosen line. Jacob's twelve sons had become the ancestors of twelve tribes, comprising a numerous people, called both Hebrews and Israelites.* They grew from tribes into a people while sojourning in Egypt, where they became enslaved. God had then performed the mighty feat of redeeming them from slavery through Moses. Further, through Moses, God had revealed the laws of living and worship by which the corporate people were to live. Just as he had revealed laws to Moses, so in subsequent ages he had revealed his will and his judgments through a succession of prophets to whom he had spoken in clear, comprehensible language.

Could the people, in the march of events, when new situations (and new dangers) arose, look to God for deeds similar to his wondrous acts against the Egyptians? In a sense, yes. But, according to the Bible, he seemed not always to respond and to intervene on behalf of his people. He allowed the Assyrians to destroy the northern kingdom in 722/21 B.C. without intervening; he allowed the Babylonians to conquer the southern kingdom in 587 B.C. and exile its inhabitants to Babylonia without

---

*A confusion exists respecting three terms, *Hebrew, Israelite, Jew.* In some usage they are interchangeable synonyms. Biblical scholars tend to use *Hebrew* for the early period of Abraham, Isaac, and Jacob; for the very next period, their term is *Israelite. Jew* is shortened from *Judean,* that is, a member of the tribe of Judah; this tribe became virtually the entire Israelite population after catastrophic events (the destruction of the northern of the Israelite kingdoms in 722 B.C. and the Babylonian exile after 587 B.C.).

Judeans perpetuated the term Israel for their collective entity, as in "Hear, O *Israel,* the Lord our God, the Lord is One." Accordingly, this became the name for the State of *Israel* after its proclamation of independence in 1948.

17

intervening. Why had he not intervened? Surely he could have, had he wanted to. Why had he not wanted to? The biblical answer was that his people had through their accumulated sins of wickedness forfeited his favor, and thereby negated his usual disposition to intervene on their behalf. Was his people more wicked than other peoples that he picked them out for targets of his divine wrath? Did he hold men and nations responsible for their deeds or misdeeds in a strict legal way, meting out severe justice to them? Was he without mercy? Or, if he could be merciful, under what conditions could he be compassionate?

It is against the background of the historical events that occurred, both the favorable and the calamitous, that the Hebrews gave their answers to the question, What is God? Their view was that he had created and ruled the world, and that he had provided men with laws and standards, and held men accountable to him. He ruled history, both the past and the future which was to unfold. He could respond to men, or else abstain from responding; he could mete out strict justice to evil-doers or else graciously pardon his sinful people. He could deal with the single individual in the same way that he dealt with the corporate body, being either scrupulously just or else graciously merciful, as seemed best to him.

He was never man's tool. He could be appealed to, as a son could appeal to a father, and he could respond or not, but he could not be *forced*. Man could appeal to him through prayer, or animal sacrifice, or through a worthy life, but man could not coerce God, for to have been able to do so would have compromised or destroyed God's godness — his omnipotence ("full power").

To the Hebrew belief, Christians appended the view that God had disclosed himself on an even higher rung of the ladder than through Abraham, Moses, and the prophets — this by sending to earth his "son" Jesus. This Jesus — described in a variety of ways as divine — had died on the cross; the death of the divine Jesus was the loving demonstration of the fullness of God's mercy, for it had made possible the redemption of men and

18

mankind without the necessity, or even the ability, on the part of man or mankind to earn this redemption. God's gift to man of the grace ("free, unearned") of redemption was the climax of the historical account of God's actions in the past and up to the present, that is, the age of early Christianity.

These assertions about God arose from the rather unique Hebraic view that God controlled the unfolding of history and that the march of historical events in turn disclosed God. The Hebrews conquered Canaan. Successively the Assyrians, the Babylonians, the Persians, the Greeks, and the Romans established world empires; God must have ordained these conquests, or at least tolerated them, and in some of the events he himself in one way or another participated, either directly or indirectly. Arising solely from an interpretation of historical events, the Hebrew belief was not framed by any extensive inquiry into sciences such as geology or astronomy. The biblical view of what God is emerged, not from an analysis of the world respecting earth, water, air, or fire, as did early Greek science, but rather out of historical events and their presumed meaning.

As mentioned above passingly, questions — profound ones — arose even for biblical man persuaded of the biblical answers. The most acute questions dealt with evil. Wicked men could prosper, and righteous suffer — Why did God allow this? Wicked nations subjected his people to conquest and persecution — How could God allow this? Biblical men wrestled with such problems, and have bequeathed to our ages stirring literature such as the Book of Job which probed into the question, How could a righteous, all powerful God allow a devastating calamity to overtake so completely righteous a man as Job?

At stake in the biblical approach is the issue of whether the events which happen to men, or to a man, are *ultimately* meaningful. No one in his right mind would deny the *influence* on subsequent time of the French Revolution, the Civil War, or the splitting of the atom. But do these (and other events) have anything to do with God? If they do not, it is quite possible that we live in a world of caprice and accident — and that would be a

19

dismal and lonely world. What the biblical view asserts is that events in history have had a significant meaning, which needs to be probed for.

Biblical man thought constantly about God, for he faced the universal problems of men: birth, growth, decline, and death. Besides, in his world there seemed an even greater abundance of mysteries than our age is ready to acknowledge, for he ascribed to God matters we would scarcely dream of. Unlike us, who prefer the science of meterology, biblical man ascribed to God the crash of thunder and the flash of lightning. God made it rain, or kept rain away; hence he caused abundant crops or the famine which resulted from drouth. From him came prosperity and adversity.

But since the sun unfailingly arose in the east and set in the west, or since offspring were born as helpless babies and not as grown persons, there were observable rules in nature. So predictable were sunrise and the helplessness of babies that one could rely fully on one's usual expectations from nature, for nature was controlled by God the creator. God implied regularity and certainty, a sense of what was assuredly bound to be. But if the rain expected in the proper season failed to come, and the crops were jeopardized, man could pray to God, but then discover that the rains still did not come. Apparently, then, God was not hearing man's prayer. Did man not pray loud enough for his prayers to rise to God's residence in the skies? Or was God asleep? Or was he away — away and unavailable, or unavailable because he was so far off? Was he near, or was he far, or where was he? In a way, he was something of a puzzle to man, for he was at times apparently near and "on the job," yet he seemed quite as often unavailable as near at hand. No tool of man, God had a way of doing things which stirred earnest questions, if not doubts, especially respecting matters which puzzled the faithful.

For the opposite phrases *unavailable* and *near at hand*, modern men have turned to words which are so useful that it is worthwhile to absorb them — the words *transcendent* and *immanent*.

What do they mean?

When biblical man spoke of God as powerful to the point that he was in control of the world, man was following a universal tendency, that of magnifying God. A first-rate God is more powerful than the winds or the sun; hence, God, to be God, must be beyond the winds, and even more distant than the sun. So far above this world is a God so magnified that in essence he is over and above it, to the point of appearing to be outside it. We call a belief in a God so magnified as to be apparently outside our world as reflecting transcendence.

But in one way, as satisfying to our egos as is our belief that our God is so great as to be beyond our world, a God so distant is at the same time unsatisfying, since our pressing needs often require a god near at hand. The term for God conceived of as near at hand is *immanent*.

Biblical man exhibits to modern analysts the diverse and simultaneous tendencies of making God transcendent and of viewing him as immanent. Since transcendent and immanent are direct opposites of each other, naturally a certain contradiction was implied. Though biblical man was less frightened of contradiction and inconsistency than we, and quite prone to harmonize these, he was acutely aware of this contradiction. At times he handled this particular contradiction simply by asserting both God's distance and his nearness.

But biblical man also turned to a number of ways of resolving the contradiction. One way, for example, was to alter his view of where God dwelled. He seems to have thought, to begin with, that God resided in a cave on the sacred mountain of the Wilderness, a mountain known both as Sinai and Horeb. When the Hebrews moved from the Wilderness into the land of Canaan, God left that mountain and moved along with them, to help them in their battles, but he altered his residence now to the heavens. Granted that this was better to believe than that God dwelled in a far away mountain cave, at the same time it made him quite distant and unavailable; the way out for biblical man is disclosed in his belief that on given sacred days, God came near, this by descending from heaven and entering the holy of holies, the inner room of the two-roomed temple which Solomon had built. These sacred days were the spring and autumn equinoxes; at dawn on those days the rays of the rising sun could enter into the Temple through its opened eastern gate, and cast no shadow on the walls. These rays represented the entry of God himself into the holy of holies, a place into which only a rare person, the high priest, might enter, and he only on infrequent occasions (it became only annual, and limited to the Day of Atonement). God, then, resided far away in heaven, but occasionally came from the distance to a holy place on earth.

For a short interval in Israelite thought, the view apparently arose that God actually resided in the Temple, rather than occasionally entering it and then leaving. That view, though, seemed to jeopardize his transcendence, and after being held for a time, it was abandoned, for it was better, in the dilemma, to have God dwell in heaven than in a man-made Temple. A biblical author, writing long after Solomon's time, depicts Solomon as proud of his accomplishment in having built the Temple, yet at the same time asserting that no building could contain God, since even the heavens were not large enough for that (I Kings 8:27).

Still another way of harmonizing the contradictory views of God's transcendence and his immanence was the rise of a belief (asserted by some to have been borrowed from Persia) in angels. *Angel* is a Greek word which means messenger; it translates a Hebrew word likewise meaning messenger. In the Bible, angels were the means of divine communication between the far-off God and man here on earth. They seem at first to have been devoid of specific personality; with the passing of time, they appear to have acquired personalities and, in the latest Hebrew biblical literature, they also acquired names such as Michael and Gabriel. (In even later times, they acquire specific job assignments. Biblical angels are considered masculine; only in recent centuries have they turned female!)

Along with the progressive growth of views of God's transcendence, there was a development in the form of the belief about his participation in the affairs of men. On the one hand, he had been portrayed in early literature as a "man of war" who himself fought in the battles, and mention is made in Numbers 21:14 of a book with the title, the Book of the Wars of the Lord; a short quotation is given from that otherwise lost ancient book.

On the other hand, his participation became conceived of not as direct and participating but, as it were, as behind the scenes; in later literature, only men are portrayed as doing the fighting, but the outcome seems to be in God's hand. Accordingly, God came to be conceived in the Bible as the invisible, latent, decisive force in the affairs of men. With God latent and invisible, yet still in full control, men could at times be quite unaware of him. They could even be unaware that they were being used by him for his purposes. Two biblical passages clearly articulate this. The arrogant Assyrian king ascribes to his own power his spectacular conquest of western lands; he is taunted (from the distance!) in these words in Isaiah 10:15: "Does the axe boast over him who wields it, the saw claim mastery over the carpenter?" No, the Assyrian is only God's tool. Second, the Persian conqueror Cyrus fashioned a great empire, but, so speaks a prophet, in full oblivion that God had summoned him for this conquest and indeed made that conquest possible (Isaiah 45:1-4).

God, then, was latent, invisible, and transcendent. An idol, made of wood or of metal, is always near at hand and visible. But an idol is not and cannot be god, for it is inanimate and able to be destroyed. Indeed, to make an idol and to worship it is to make a mockery of true divinity and was (so it was believed) a horrible disrespect of God. For God, in the matured view in the Hebrew Bible, is not a man-made idol; he is not visible, he is not tangible, he is not in a literal way involved in the humdrum affairs of man.

This conclusion I have termed the matured view; there is no scarcity of biblical passages in which God is visible, or can take dust of the earth and fashion man, and the like. In part, these passages reflect an early stage in the long growth of biblical thought. On the other hand (to revert to a matter mentioned above, page 13, the way of speaking about God), one must make allowance for the *manner* of biblical narration, as exemplified in the redemption of the Hebrews from slavery in Egypt. The biblical narrative presents two themes side by side, the one theme centering in Moses and what that great man did, and the other centering in God's close guidance of Moses to the extent that Moses is relatively unimportant, for it is really God who is acting. Thus the purely human account is overlaid by elements of literal, direct divine participation. Perhaps the two themes, what man did and what God did, are at most a reflection of a purely literary device, the net effect of which could quite reasonably be put in this way: The Hebrews were enslaved in Egypt and brought to freedom by Moses, but behind the scenes, it was actually God, not Moses, acting; in the centuries in which the account was transmitted, it came to be the manner of writing to put God directly on stage from time to time.

There is no important issue in this matter of the manner of writing the enslavement story, for it is beyond question that the ultimate view in the Bible is that God, not Moses, rescued the Hebrews. Thus, a transcendent God exhibited his immanence in the great event of the release from slavery, as he did in other historical events. God himself rescued; an idol could not. God had intervened in Egypt out of his pity for the suffering of the Hebrews.

We need now to pick up again that most important distinction set forth earlier between knowledge and belief. By and large we can *know* about historical events. We can often call on archeology or documents in archives to buttress and confirm our knowledge of historical events. We can *know* about the Hebrew conquest of Canaan, or the Assyrian empire, or the Persian.

But respecting God's control of the Hebrew forces or of the Assyrian or Persian monarchs, or of his guidance of a Moses in the enslavement in Egypt, we are in the realm of belief, not knowledge. Granted that occasionally some biblical events are described in a confusing way (as today witnesses of an automo-

24

bile accident may give different versions), nevertheless, there is a sense in which most of the historical events of the Bible are verifiable. The role ascribed to God in the Bible, however, is in the domain of belief, not of knowledge. Archeologists can prove the Assyrian conquest; it is not possible to prove that God designed it, planned it, and executed his plan. Historians can document the rise of the Persian empire, but not that God provided the Persian king Cyrus with his victories.

Now, it is as legitimate to ask about World War II — Was this something God has guided? — as it is to ask it about the westward march of Assyria. We do not know; we can believe, or we can disbelieve. The biblical authors have recorded their beliefs, not their knowledge.

We, too, can either believe or not believe about God, whether in the biblical accounts or in the events of our own time.

VI

Some Routes to the Belief in God

IF GOD IS invisible, intangible, and latent in the course of his
torical events, and if belief or disbelief are our only options
can we amplify all this in some way so that we can move a bi
beyond these bare options?

We must here turn to three items: sacred literature, man'
ability to reason, and the matter of human experience.

Who wrote the Bible — God or men? What stakes are there ir
the question? Is the Bible only edifying literature, possibly in qual
ity beyond Shakespeare, but still quite kindred to him? Or does
the Bible have a divine origin that the most ardent lover of
Shakespeare would never attribute to him?

What makes sacred literature sacred is the conviction, held ir
the Religions, that God is the ultimate author of the Bible. One
says ultimate author, for the reason that certain biblical books
carry the name of humans, such as Isaiah or Amos. Judaism and
Christianity, however, have deemed these men in some way to
be in touch with God and motivated or even guided by him ir
their writing.

The origin of the belief in the divine authorship of the Bible
seems to lie in a passage in the Book of Exodus, 32:16: "The
tablets [of the Ten Commandments] were the work of God,
the writing was God's etched on the tablets." Another passage
Deuteronomy 10:9, speaks of "the two stone tablets written by
the finger of God."

Other passages, indeed many of them, speak of Moses having
written his laws, as God had revealed these to him. An extension

was made in the historic Religions beyond the explicit, divine authorship of the Ten Commandments in the following way: Moses had indeed written his laws, but he had done so, as it were, by taking down some divine dictation, so that in effect God was the real author of the Five Books seemingly written by Moses.

By further extension, books bearing names such as Isaiah and Amos also appeared to reflect divine dictation, for in these books God is portrayed as having spoken to these men.

Accordingly, so the belief has been, no matter how individualistic a particular biblical book may seem to be respecting the humanity of its author, all biblical books were spurred by God, and the human aspect involved in their writing relatively unimportant. But, to turn things about now, it is a fact that a great many books were in good circulation among the Jews (and at a later time among Christians). However, only those few books were admitted into the Bible (during its largely unknown process of formation) which merited a common assent that God had been involved in the writing. Jews and Christians did not exclude "divine" books from the Bible; the excluded books, many surviving to our time in part or in full, failed to gain recognition as divine.

On what basis has the divine origin of biblical books been commended to modern men? Usually on the basis that authentic tradition, handed down unbrokenly from generation to generation has asserted this, and the tradition has been credible. Moreover, if one pressed backward in time, the first contention of the divine origin of some ancient biblical writing arose from eyewitnesses either of the events themselves or from eyewitnesses of the writing about the events. The historic Religions thus have preserved and perpetuated not only the books themselves but also very ancient contentions about the original writing of them. Respecting Christian books, for example, we are informed by a fourth century writer (who is quoting a second century bishop) that Mark wrote his Gospel in Rome, from the recollections of Jesus' disciple Peter, whose secretary Mark was; Matthew, ac-

27

cording to this same bishop, was a disciple of Jesus and, hence, an eyewitness of the events he wrote about in his Gospel.

The direct biblical statements about the divine writing of the Ten Commandments, and then the extension of this, inferentially, to include all the Five Books of Moses, and, thereafter, the legacy of books such as Isaiah and Amos which report communicable conversation with God, should account to us for the way in which the Bible has come to be conceived in the Religions as sacred, with sacred in this sense simply meaning divine.

Derived views proceeded to suggest that since God is the epitome of truth, the Bible too is "truth." And since manifestly God — in order to be God — could never make a mistake, the Bible is free from all error — even in such fields of study unknown in ancient times as geology or astrophysics.

A person persuaded by the view of the church or synagogue he belongs to that the Bible is divine, and sacred and free of error, naturally considers the biblical account of God's activities in ancient times fully credible. For the person who believes in the divine origin of the Bible, the question, What is God? is not too difficult to answer (though even for him also it is not a completely simple matter).

But at an opposite extreme is the opinion, an essentially eighteenth century one, that it was men, not God, who wrote the Bible. Moreover, a procedure of study for the Bible was suggested at that time which had arisen from the study of classical Greek and Roman literature. Did "Homer" write the Iliad and the Odyssey, all of each at one given time? Or did these epics grow out of oral tradition and become recorded not by one man, Homer, but by a succession of men over many generations? Whereas religious tradition ascribed the Pentateuch to Moses, careful study (begun in the eighteenth, but brought to a high point in the nineteenth century) suggested that the Pentateuch reflected four different levels of writing, distinct and separable from each other. The earliest of the four levels was written some four to five centuries after the age of Moses, and the youngest of the four at least a thousand years after his age; hence, the

28

Five Books of Moses could not have been written by Moses. Also, the Book of Isaiah shows some portions near the end to be the writings of a man who lived two hundred years after the man with whose writings the Book of Isaiah begins. The Book of Isaiah is not entirely by "Isaiah." The last verses of Amos seem clearly an appendage to the book; the Book of Amos is not entirely by "Amos."

What the Religions told about the authorship of biblical books was set aside by many learned men as untenable.

As for errors, a man free of the assumptions in the Religions of the "inerrancy" of Scripture, could point to at least three frequent types of errors in the Bible. One type is illustrated with Cain's wife. The entire population at one time consisted of Adam and Eve and their two sons, Cain and Abel. When Cain killed Abel, the population shrank to three. Where, then, did Cain get the wife by whom he begot the long line of descendants mentioned in Genesis 4:17-24?

There is a second type of error. The list of the descendants just mentioned appears to be repeated in Genesis 5:6-27, but with these differences: that the forbear is not Cain, but Seth, his brother, born to Adam and Eve after Cain's murder of Abel. Certain names in these two lists are absolutely identical; other names appear to be the same, though spelled slightly differently (as we can call a girl Katherine, Cathryn, or Kate, or Katie). Why two lists, and discrepancies in the spellings, and discrepancies about who begot whom — this in the light of the "inerrancy" of Scripture? Why also is there a whole host of double, or even triple accounts of some items, presented with details so divergent as to defy honest reconciliation? Again, why is the enslavement in Egypt, in one passage, four hundred years in length, in another four hundred and thirty, and in other passages a period of at most three generations — this in a book free of error?

And why do the Gospels exhibit contradictions within a single Gospel, and greater contradictions as between one Gospel (such as Mark) and another (such as Matthew)?

God could scarcely err. Since the Bible contains errors — and men unlike God can certainly err — it was concluded that men had written the Bible.

If the question is asked, in what domains of society does the view that men wrote the Bible reside, the answer is this: among scholars of Bible and the clergy (Catholic, Protestant, and Jewish). Indeed, inner denominational divisions as between "modernist" and "fundamentalist" arose in the churches mostly in the nineteenth century, and primarily from the issue of the origin of the Bible, whether from God or man.

The further question can arise: Do the scholars and the clergy who accept either a completely human origin, or at least some sort of human origin, of the Bible extend it to the point of denying totally that God is in some way discernible in it? The answer is, No, they do not. They differ among themselves on what might be called "quantity," that is, how much of the admittedly human Bible they go on to believe is divine. In a general way, such scholars and clergy admit the presence of "errors," contradictions, and other problems in the Bible, but, to use words I do not find them using, it is the errors that reflect the human aspect; beyond this admitted human aspect, the voice of God is still audible in Scripture. Though the Book of Isaiah is divisible into at least two parts, and Amos has indeed been extended by an addition, and Matthew differs radically from Mark, these writings, so it is held, nevertheless echo the voice of God.

The non-fundamentalists are often divisible into two camps, the difference being largely one of degree. There are middle-of-the-roaders, who feel that honesty compels using the results of modern biblical scholarship, but not to the point that its sanctity is entirely dissolved. The extremists (some of whom are scholarly clergy in the historic churches) are quite unrestrained about biblical scholarship, but they are not thereby moved to detach themselves from their historic churches.*

*The clergy of most urban churches and synagogues in the United States do not believe about the Bible what most of their parishioners think they do, or

30

The moderates, that is the conservatives, represent minds able at the same time to concede a human aspect to Scripture, but still to attribute to it a sanctity and authority almost equal to that which fundamentalists attribute. The liberals and extremists, on the other hand, usually manage to be selective, and to attribute sanctity and authority to selected portions of Scripture (they can seem to be doing so capriciously!) or to manage to salvage some vestige of authority for Scripture. The religious mind is elastic, and quite capable of stretching points without any awareness of the stretching.

In denominations such as the Unitarian-Universalist, or the (Hicksite) Quakers, or Reform Judaism, there are to be found clergy who have been decisively influenced by biblical scholarship. Elsewhere, the laity seems seldom to suspect that its intuitive doubts or questions about the divine origin of Bible are matched by the doubts that their clergy have been instructed in. Again to the question of what is God in the Bible, conservatives and liberals will often resort to a clerical cliche: The Bible is not the word of God, but the word of God is in the Bible.

This sort of thing is a form of "special pleading" and not a consequence of deliberate or acknowledged dishonesty, but rather the bond necessary to a clergyman between the chore he has personally undertaken for himself and the Religion he fits into. When such clergy speak about God, they are not reflecting accurately what is in the Bible, but giving their own worthy or idiosyncratic adaptations of it. They tell us what *they* think about God, not about what God is. If we are not fundamentalists, we can expect no secure, verifiable knowledge about God from the usual clergy.

●

---

should, believe. No deliberate deception on the part of such clergy is involved. On the Sabbath they read from Scripture and preach from it, as if no issue of the divine or human origin exists. In weeknight Bible classes, they will usually use the scholarship they do not use on the Sabbath, for its use on the Sabbath would intrude into the worship service.

This last statement is not meant to be sensational or shocking — or a disparagement. It is, indeed, an inevitable answer, and it can apply, as we shall now see, even to fundamentalists, when they, like modernists, stray into the history of the philosophy of religion.

But here we must pause for a definition. Ideally, philosophy is an inquiry into the nature of man and the universe devoid of conscious antecedent suppositions. The philosopher is at his best when he tries, without any presuppositions of any kind, to discover by inquiry what the truth is. The philosophy of religion is a different matter. It is an inquiry into the truth of the presuppositions of religion, or of a Religion, by using aspects of the manner of inquiry of the free philosopher. The free philosopher could conceivably say, "I am neither a believer nor an atheist. I shall search for an answer to the question, 'Is there a God?' as honestly, openly, and profoundly as I can." The philosopher of religion would say, "I am a believer (Jew, Christian, Muslim). I believe in God. I shall now seek to confirm this belief as honestly, openly, and profoundly as I can."*

Philosophy in the western world was born among the Greeks. Greeks and Jews encountered each other at the times of the world conquest by Alexander the Great about 325 B.C. In subsequent ages, they borrowed from each other, both in matters of folklore and folk-practices, but also in matters of philosophy. (Some Jews, and many early Christians — Paul, for example — scorned Greek philosophy.) The "philosophy of religion" received its initial major formulation at the hands of a Jew, Philo of Alexandria (20 B.C. to A.D. 40), who "explained" the Judaism to which he was ardently loyal by utilizing Plato and the Stoics. Medieval Muslim, Christian, Jewish philosophy has similarly "reconciled" the ancestral faith, though often preferring to use Aristotle rather than Plato or the Stoics.

*A thin line of demarcation exists between "philosophy of religion" and theology; see page x. It may be put in this way, that theology begins with the affirmations of a Religion, while philosophy of religion seeks for bases on which such affirmation might be made.

A latent paradox marks all such philosophers (and theologians). Their fidelity to the Religions was stressed above. Yet the resort to the manner of philosophy, exemplified both in Philo and in the medieval thinkers, led to an acknowledgment that *man can make no affirmative substantial statements about God*, such as "God is just" or "God watches over mankind." This kind of statement cannot reasonably be made, because such a statement *defines* God. The word *define* includes the Latin root *fin*, which means limit, so that *to define God* is in effect to limit him; yet the inherent religious assumption about God has always been that, as omnipotent, he is without limit. Therefore, since even the affirmations logically limit God, the philosophers have concluded that such affirmations about God cannot be made. They adopted a different procedure; if men could not make affirmations about God, this inability did not preclude man's making negative statements. Thus, instead of saying God is just, or God watches over mankind, one might proceed to say: God is *not* unjust; or, God does *not* abstain from watching over mankind.

The significance of all this for the modern thinking person is that, insofar as science and logic are utilized, God always remains unknowable, for the simple reason that his domain is the area which is beyond man's knowledge and beyond man's proving. We cannot by philosophy know what God is.

Now, a poor yet enlightening analogy from the field of medicine is available which can possibly narrow what we are talking about, and, one hopes, clarify it. (It is a poor analogy because it breaks down at a given point, as we shall see.) The analogy is with the common cold. No one would deny that the common cold exists. We are all familiar with aspects of what it does: it weakens us, it causes us discomfort, it can develop into a severe and very dangerous illness. So far, however, medical science cannot explain the direct cause of the common cold.

The inability to explain the cause of the common cold in no way removes the common cold from human experience. Without our knowing the direct cause, we can still know the effects.

In somewhat the same way, though we cannot *know* God by means of philosophy, we can still be aware of the effects of God. Philo of Alexandria has a somewhat complicated way of illustrating the difference between actually knowing God and knowing the *effects*, as it were. In his judgment, a man of even the lowest mentality can be aware that creation has taken place, for he sees the results of creation in the world of land and waters, trees and fish. A man of somewhat higher mentality can notice the regularity in the parade of the seasons, in that spring precedes summer, not summer spring; the sun rises in the east, not the west; this man of somewhat higher mentality can be aware that in some way the world seems to be "governed." The man of still higher mentality can discover a somewhat deeper orderliness in the world, in that an apple seed grows into an apple tree, not a pear tree, and certain medications exercize predictable effects on the person who takes them; from this latter circumstance, one can conclude that the orderliness in the world is the result of some superhuman intelligence. So Philo.

Philo has a striking terminology by which he expresses these things. What is knowable, according to Philo, are the clear results of the existence of God; there are knowable facets, knowable aspects, of his unknowable essence, his unknowable "fullness." Philo was willing to speak of one such knowable facet as "the Creative Power" of God. That Creative Power, in Philo's view, does not exhaust God, but describes only one divine activity, the result of which a man can actually know, simply by looking around him at land and water, which were "created." The man of somewhat higher mentality can speak of "the Ruling Power" of God (that spring precedes summer), and thereby express still another knowable facet of the unknowable totality, God's rule. An even better mind, probing more deeply than these two types, discovers aspects of the intelligence by which the world operates, as in the case of apple seeds and the apple tree. Accordingly, while Philo insists that philosophically God is unknowable, he is quite ready to describe the higher intelligence by which the world operates as having a real existence.

But God himself is unknowable.

I said that the analogy of the common cold is a poor one, and breaks down. Philosophically, God must always be unknowable; hopefully the cause of the common cold will some day become known.

Perhaps by now one might say that a statement which I often encounter in living rooms, which equates God with some old man with a white beard sitting up in heaven, is disclosed as a frivolous, superficial kind of statement. It is to be excused because religious schools sometimes convey just this kind of thing to children, and these children, on becoming adults, seem to abide by this childish portrayal as if it were the conviction even of mature people.

What is God? We do not know; we cannot know. The Bible tells us its *belief*, and we can accept or reject it. If we do not regard the Bible as divine, the Bible is telling us (profoundly, cogently) only what certain men believed, not what those men know. The philosophers do not help us, for, themselves not knowing, they cannot tell us.

Have we lost God? No; at most we have lost only a historically important way of conceiving him and of speaking about him and about our possible beliefs.

To whom do we need to tell what we believe? Surely only ourselves. For that we may indeed be helped if we borrow biblical or philosophical words. Yet we might be just as well off without any borrowing, for we can speak to ourselves silently, without words.

●

There is a third matter (as we said above), man's experience. Two of us may read the same book, see the same picture, hear the same music; one of us is bored and the other deeply moved. If we are moved, we may be able, or unable, to say why we are moved, but the recourse to explaining why we are moved comes

35

after the experience. Whether we can explain or not, the experience of having been deeply moved is a personal reality.

In the realm of living, where the joy of births or the sorrow of deaths touch us, or fear and acute anxiety shatter us, two of us may undergo the same affirmative or negative events, and one of us be cold and blasé and the other deeply moved — moved to the point that he feels that for the moment, however, passingly, he has somehow been touched by something beyond the mere incident itself. That something he can tell himself, or someone else, is God. This experience is also a personal reality.

That is to say, God can be experienced — this as distinct from one's being taught about the Bible in religious school or being told what was thought about him by the philosophers.

While it is certainly true that some people have been deluded about having experienced God, this fact of the clear delusion of some in no way negates the personal reality of the experience to them, or to those we might agree are undeluded.

I will discuss this in fuller detail in the chapter on Mysticism. Here I limit myself to this observation, that in the history of the human race, it has more usually been a sense of the *experience* of God rather than the teachings of the Bible or the wisdom of the philosophers that have impinged on men.

How can we guard against delusion? Belief, I have said, is different from knowing; belief enters in *after* available knowledge is exhausted.

Now, knowledge is not exhausted if man does not use it; belief legitimately arises when a person knows all that can be known, not before. Belief legitimately arises when we have tested and challenged and made certain what can be known.

Sometimes belief is credible, sometimes not. If the prerequisite stage of previous knowledge is fraught with error, I cannot reasonably use it as a basis for legitimate belief. If, in the middle of the night, with a full moon shining, I say that I believe it is noon, then I am flying in the face of ready facts and am being deluded (and deceiving even myself); my delusion might consist, too, in my futile playing with words, as if noon can mean some-

36

thing other than noon. My belief must arise *after* my supposed knowledge has been squared with the facts and not *without* the facts or *against* the facts. In the matter of God, if my astronomy or geology or history are wrong, then I can scarcely move from such wrong knowledge into tenable belief.

If a belief chances to arise prior to the recourse to knowledge, then subsequent recourse to it can readily destroy the belief. Only after we have made certain about knowledge and clearly seen its limits can we justly proceed into belief. Delusion arises from incomplete knowledge or faulty knowledge, or from ignoring knowledge. A belief which flies in the face of genuine knowledge is only a whim, that and nothing more.

But a belief when requisite knowledge precedes it is not a whim; to believe is a defensible step to take when adequate knowledge is insufficient for the answers one seeks.

If we believe in what we know to be false, we can momentarily satisfy ourselves, but we then face the almost inevitable certainty of the discovery of the falseness of that knowledge and the loss of our belief. (Most of us who "lose" our religion do so because what we were taught as children became disclosed to us as falsity when we moved out of childhood.)

An emotional experience is a delusion if it arises from wrong knowledge or prematurely from an absence of it. The person who rejoices at a school examination he thinks he will get an A on, or who despairs at having flunked, ought reasonably wait until he gets his grade before he rejoices or despairs.

Some of us are tone-deaf and cannot respond to music. Others of us cannot respond to art or to literature. Others of us, the most impoverished of all people, cannot respond to the mystery of living.

To experience God, as it were, can be a personal reality and at the same time a complete delusion. Yet if such an experience ensues after knowledge, even though it may remain a personal reality, it is not based on falseness.

Naturally, a person who does not accept, in some way, that God exists can scarcely experience him. To repeat, in the history

37

of the race, God, as it were, has become a reality to men more through personal emotional experience than through what men have been taught about him by other men.

But God as an experience does not disclose what God is, for the experience does not proceed that far. In sum, every one fashions his individual belief about what God is — his own personal God.

But here we need to avoid a confusion, for we can hear someone say, "My *personal* God is a loving father"; another will say, "I cannot believe in a *personal* God." The word personal is used in different senses in the two sentences. In the first, "personal" refers to the ideas, views, norms that characterize not God but the speaker in much the same way that one can say, "I have my own doctor, my personal physician; I do not go to anonymous doctors in a clinic."

In the other use, a personal God is a phrase suggesting that God is more than just a vague force, disconnected from all time and place; the intent, rather, is to suggest that just as a man has qualities of size, age, place of residency, so too God has them — we must here remember that we can speak of God only by using ordinary human terms we do not actually mean, as observed on page 13. Perhaps to think of the opposite of a personal God, as expressed in pantheism, is enlightening. The word *pantheism* means "God is everywhere, in everything." He permeates all nature, indeed the entire universe, and he is free from allocation, as it were, to place and time. By and large, the Religions have espoused the view of God as a person in the sense of specific characteristics, and they have considered pantheism (advocated by the seventeenth century philosopher Spinoza) as an offensive error or even a heresy. God as a person is the opposite of a pantheistic God.

When a person chooses either pantheism or a "personal" God, he is in the domain of belief, as are the Religions.

Is there an objective reality in an experience of God, or is it only subjective? Who can say? Two people can hear the same music, and one is moved and the other is not. Which is real? There is more to say, and later I say it.

38

VII

Man

WE HEAR WORDS such as soul, spirit, conscience, but often they are used so very, very loosely as to seem meaningless. Moreover, ancient writers have used *soul* and *spirit* interchangeably in various diverse settings, and thereby have blunted their precise import. While I shall presently define the words, the reader should be more concerned with the ideas involved than with the words themselves.

We can begin to understand soul and spirit, as the ancient Hebrews did, by a contrast of the two with the body. The body is the physical, tangible part of men; it consists of flesh, of bones, of fingernails and toenails and of hair. Soul and spirit are the opposite; they are intangible.

First, *soul*. What shall we mean by it? In answer, there is a sense in which, when awake, I am conscious. That part of me able to be conscious is my soul. Within this domain of consciousness there is also my mind, with which I am (possibly) able to think; also within the domain of the soul is the issue of how I respond to moral challenges and to matter relating to conscience, that is, the issue of how I assess "right" and "wrong."

Spirit is by etymology derived from the Latin word for breath, as is the case with the Hebrew term for it. A living person breathes, a dead person does not. Hence, spirit is the facet of man which is alive, the facet which makes the body living. Different kinds of breath can infuse me. If I am drunk, it is the breath of drunkenness. If I am insane, it is the breath of insanity. My spirit, then, is the living part of me which describes those

39

characteristics of mine which are not purely physical. If I am generous, I have a "generous spirit"; if mean, a "mean spirit." Spirit, then, describes my personality so long as I live.

(Let me comment passingly that biblical man observed people or animals who bled to death; hence at times he defined being alive by "blood" rather than by spirit. Again, not yet knowing what we have managed to learn since those days, he attributed the seat of the intelligence to the heart, and the seat of the emotions to the liver, rather than the soul.)

How can we proceed to distinguish between soul and spirit? We can observe that animals breathe but do not seem to think, or to reason, or to possess consciences; we can attribute spirit to them but not soul. We speak of a race horse as "high-spirited" and a work animal as having "sluggish spirit."

If I am asked to describe some person, I might focus on his or her height or weight (that is, his or her body); usually I would talk about personal traits — quick or slow, intelligent or dull, responsive or unresponsive, altruistic or self-centered. My description would focus more on the intangibles than on the body; in effect, I would be speaking about the *spirit* of a person.

Ancient man assumed that a person became the kind of person that he was in consequence of the kind of spirit which infused him. Indeed, in the sense that we too can describe a person and ignore his physique, our description can be of a person's "spirit." We, however, would mean this only figuratively, whereas ancient man often supposed that a person was an actual blend of his physical body and of his "spirit," as if two separable entities had become intertwined. They understood the body as solid; spirit, though not solid, was nevertheless something discernible, almost tangible, as my visible breath can be on a cold day. That I can move my hand through my breath on a cold day reveals to me the unsolid nature of breath. It seemed to differ from the body in the matter of solidness.

It followed for ancient man that, if body and spirit had become blended, the two could in turn become separable. If in a dream we see someone dead, it is his spirit we dream about, his spirit separated from his body. Stories in the Bible of the summoning of a man from the grave, as the witch of Endor summoned Samuel (1 Samuel 28:3-20) meant calling up his spirit not his body. The spirit, though tangible but not solid, appeared to ancient man as its own kind of individual entity.

Spirit, then, relates to the individual characteristic of man, indeed to his individuality as a living, breathing entity. Soul, never becoming visible like breath on a cold day, relates to his consciousness, to his mind and its functions, to conscience and the like. Soul in Greek is *psyche*, the mind, and from this word comes the term psychology. The way in which a man's soul operates becomes the clue to his spirit. Reciprocally, his spirit can affect the manner in which his soul works.

Since psyche encompasses mind, it is evident that among men there are minds of different quality, just as there are different degrees of quality between men and animals. When a dog sees a bone and walks to it, his sight of the bone has entered into his mind, and his mind has directed his feet to walk to the bone. Now, that set of related actions is different in quality from the mind of a man when he reasons that the hypotenuse of a right triangle is the square root of the sums of the squares of the two sides. A dog does not do that. Ancient psychologists spoke of the lower mind (that of the dog that sees the bone) and of an added dimension which man possesses (enabling him to deal with triangles) called the *higher mind*. (Later on in time, the term *animal mind* was used for what earlier was called the *lower mind*.)

A distinction that was made was along this line: the lower mind of a man (like the mind of a dog) functioned, strictly and only, in the realm of the five senses: sight, hearing, smell, taste, and touch. The higher mind functioned beyond them, namely, in the realm of abstractions and not in the realm of the senses. Man's lower mind can lead on to the higher: it is by means of our lower mind that we see apples on a tree and go to pick one; it is by means of our higher mind that we formulate general conclusions about apples (they are fruit, not animals) or trees

41

they are organic, not stone). The lower mind can reason only in direct relationship with the senses; the higher mind can go beyond the achievements of the senses and call on a higher reason to formulate general conclusions not directly bound to the senses. The lower mind never deals with such abstractions as justice, beauty, or decency; these are the province of the higher mind. Soul and higher mind are intimately related.

Other aspects can now come before us, for example, memory and conscience. It should be unnecessary to define memory. Conscience, though, needs explanation. We revert to the dog and the bone; if the dog has just eaten two or three pounds of beef, and then sees the bone, he may prefer to ignore it. In terms of the *psyche*, he has not felt driven by one of the passions which the Greeks classified as four: lust, hunger, sorrow, joy. The passion for food falls under lust, as does the sexual urge. If I have a passion for food, or for a woman, I may recklessly obey that passion. If I am aware that I pay a price in obesity through overeating, or in the future entanglements that could arise from pursuing that woman, I may persuade myself to desist; if that happens, my higher mind has so asserted itself as to control my passion.

Suppose, though, that I know that no entanglements with that woman will ensue, but that I have been so reared as to suppose that I should stay away from her because she is someone else's wife; for me to have her, even though there will be no entanglements, is simply wrong. Conscience is that part of our consciousness which speaks to us of right and wrong.

Ancient psychologists spoke of the *elenchos*, which acts as a restrainer of passions; modern psychology speaks of a *super-ego* which acts to restrain the natural passions of the *id*.

By soul, then, we shall mean that aspect of man which is involved in his reasoning, in his abstractions, his consciousness, his conscience. Perhaps laboriously, we can now conclude that the point at which soul and spirit become similar to the point of identity is where the results of one person's complex soul becomes a way of describing his spirit, his personality.

A passage in a modern Jewish prayer book blends the two matters, soul and spirit, together in these words:

> My God, the soul which thou hast given me came pure from thee. Thou hast created it, thou hast formed it, thou hast breathed it into me, and, at the appointed time, thou shalt take it from this body.

The phrase "and breathed it into me" is really more applicable to spirit than to the soul — but we need not linger over this loose use of words, except to see that the words *soul* and *spirit* have often come to be used interchangeably.

People die; they cease to breathe; they cease to reason. Clearly, the body has died; indeed, it is normally buried (today the practice of cremation seems on the increase). At death, though, what happens to the soul or to the spirit? Is it possible that the soul or the spirit lives on even after the body dies? If there had not been on the part of ancient man a distinction between body on the one hand and soul-spirit on the other the question would not have arisen.

Modern man can legitimately ask, How truly separable are body and soul-spirit? At the death, does the soul-spirit also perish? Or is death only the occasion when the separation of body and soul-spirit takes place?

He may also ask, If death means the separation from each other of body and soul-spirit, when did the two coalesce? — at impregnation, or during fetal development, or at birth?

Does the soul-spirit, possessing, as it were, personality traits, exist separately? Does it, a separate thing, enter the body, as at birth, and then leave the body, as at death?

Modern men in general incline to view the supposition of separable body and soul-spirit as an unreal, only a theoretical opinion. Body and soul-spirit are indeed viewed as different aspects of man, but only analytically; in actuality the differences are not viewed as "real."

In the Hebrew Bible, the dominant view was "unitary," namely, that body and soul-spirit were not truly separable entities. In the Greek world, a "dualism" prevailed, suggesting that they were indeed two distinct entities. In Plato's famous figure of speech, the soul was a prisoner within the body, expressed in a Greek pun: *soma* ("body") is a *sema* ("prison").

In religious terms, it is primarily the soul-spirit which is viewed as coming into relation with God. This is so because men differ from each other more respecting soul-spirit than they do respecting body, since all bodies are pretty much alike in function. When a man does an evil thing, such as killing another man, even though his hand may have done the killing, the culpable part of this man is his soul-spirit. Hence, Religions ordinarily deal with body in only a secondary way; in religion it is the soul-spirit which truly indicates the qualities of an individual, the qualities that bring him into relationship with God.

In ancient times, the body, when uncontrolled, was viewed as able to alienate man from God. It was the soul-spirit that God was viewed as potentially or actually connected with, and by soul and spirit the alienation from him overcome.

The general (though not the total) trend in the Religions has been to devaluate the body, and to despise its functions. This has been the case more in the Greek religious traditions than in the Hebrew, but the Hebrew tradition too has had its restricted devaluations. The extremes in devaluation are exemplified in the matter of religious fasts and of continence or celibacy, on the premise that the starving of the body in some way contributes to elevating the soul. Indeed, at different times, and in various traditions, it has seemed to some men highly desirable completely to "mortify" the body, not only by depriving it of adequate sustenance or release, but even by resorting to such things as sleeping on a bed of nails.

Soul and spirit in the Religions, then, are more than merely the analysis of what man is; they are the aspects of man which determine his religious rightness or wrongness. The usual frames of reference have been these, that the body is by assumption prone to be impure; the issue is whether a person is able to shield his soul or spirit from the impurity apt to derive from his impure body.

There are strands in some Religions which view sexual relations as impure. In some, also, there is a supposition (for example) that a woman's menstrual flow, or even her bearing of a child, defiles her; this is the case in traditional Judaism. Hence, an Orthodox synagogue has often had a *miqve* ("pool of water") so that a woman, immersing herself in conformity with a prescribed ritual, sheds her impurity. In traditional Christian thought, a baby inherits "original sin," that is, inherited guilt — more about this later — and requires baptism to be redeemed from the "taint" of inherited guilt.

How broadly modern men have rebelled against the view of the body and its functions as essentially impure, I am unable to say. Certainly much of nineteenth and twentieth century literature reflects what seems to me such a broad rebellion, especially in urban, middle class people. There has been virtually no theoretical rebellion against the usual decencies of honesty and kindliness; a generation ago it was customary for "non-religious" people to assert that their religion was the "golden rule." The depth, if not the breadth, of the revolt in the area of human behavior has been a repudiation of the notion that the body, and hence sex, is evil. Men have seriously questioned whether the soul-spirit is indeed separable from the body, and whether the essential person is susceptible of contamination by however unrestrained his gratification of his body might be.

Men do not (or should not!) question that there is such a thing as the mind, or consciousness, or conscience. We can know that these do exist.

Whether the soul-spirit is a separate entity in the religious sense, and answerable to God, is a matter of belief, not knowledge. Judaism and Christianity historically have affirmed that this is the case. Whether one chooses to accept this belief or not is dependent on a quite larger array of considerations. It becomes bound up with what a person also believes about sin, and about what happens to the individual after death. The key to these other beliefs arises from the observance that there are indeed the two aspects of man, his material body and the part of him which is differentiable from the body.

45

VIII

Sin and Guilt

MODERN MAN HAS difficulties in many ways in understanding sin. This is because standards have changed, and what was once viewed as sin often is no longer so viewed, as we shall see. Moreover, sin and crime become confused.

Let us begin with the simplest of trial explanations: a sin is a trespass against God*; a crime is a trespass against a human government. At points sin and crime overlap. For a Jew to steal is both to sin and to commit a crime. For a Jew to eat pork (if he is Orthodox) is a sin, but not a crime. For a Roman Catholic to become divorced, or to practice birth control, is a sin, but not a crime. For a Jewish or Christian youngster to refuse to register for the military draft is a crime, but hardly a sin.

There is no such thing as sin to be envisaged except on the sup-

---

*The term *ethical monotheism* is often used in brief description of Judaism, Christianity, and Islam. In the ancient Hebrew religion there were two aspects involved in fidelity to God. One was the obligation to a loyalty exclusive to him; it meant not worshipping any other God. The second aspect was the view that God had commanded men to observe ethical standards and even specific rules in their dealings with fellowmen; hence, he who violated such ethics by his social misbehavior was thereby disobedient to God. Indeed, we might put it in this way, that the essence of religion was man's loyalty to God and the substance of that essence was man's duty to his fellowman.

That ethics was so intrinsically interwoven with the view of God distinguished the Hebrew religion either mostly or even entirely from other ancient religions; in the others, matters of ethics were not viewed as so deeply related to religion. Hence, the term *ethical monotheism* describes briefly this Hebrew distinctiveness, preserved in Judaism, Christianity, and Islam.

46

position that God's demand on man has antecedently been specified, for if a sin is a trespass against God, presumably it is known what God requires or prohibits. The ancient Hebrews provided a quick, learnable digest of God's requirements in the form of the Ten Commandments.

Our modern difficulty can become clearer if we look at two of these: "Thou shalt not steal." Stealing can be both a crime and a sin. But suppose that in economic depression and unemployment, a man, out of his anguish that his children are starving, steals a loaf of bread. Surely on the face of it he has committed both a sin and a crime. Would we want him punished? Do we condemn him, or do we consider him to have been right to have stolen? Or what do we think?

Again, a wealthy woman suffers from kleptomania, an uncontrollable compulsion to steal. She has stolen a handtowel at a department store, worth fifty cents. She has six dozen of legally purchased handtowels in a closet at her home; she did not need the towel she stole. Shall we say she is a sinner and a criminal? Or shall we say, instead, that she is sick? Do we want her fined or, for an unnecessary theft, jailed? Or do we want her to get psychiatric help? When does an act cease to reflect crime and sin, and reflect only mental illness?

"Thou shalt not commit adultery." First, we should understand a legal distinction; fornication is a person's illicit sex act with a partner who is unmarried, while adultery involves a partner married to someone else. It is adultery which Old and New Testaments prohibit; the prohibition of fornication is a matter only of recent centuries.

Do we today regard adultery as a sin? Or is it only an unimportant indiscretion — or not even an indiscretion, but rather a legitimate privilege?

One aspect of our difficulty in understanding sin is that by and large we today exempt certain acts that historically were thought to be sin, such as homosexuality, or divorce among Christians. Indeed, often today people seem inclined to suppose that sin no longer exists! This is the case not only because modern men im-

47

plicitly or explicitly reject the supposition of a divine mandate for human conduct, but also that, while possibly accepting the thought of a divine mandate, they moderate its absolute character by treating it as susceptible of being relative. Do not steal — unless compelled to do so!

Or, perhaps the secularization of our day accounts for the fading of sin from modern awareness. That is, when trespasses like stealing become recorded in state law codes as crimes, the religious aspects have become secondary or else have disappeared entirely. If stealing has become a governmental problem, it can seem to be no longer a religious one. Again, the total array of sins enumerated in the Five Books of Moses includes matters of ancient ritual so far removed from our ken that we are loath to continue to view as sins such biblical trespass as any physical contact with a corpse or with a menstruous woman. Sin is not what it used to be!

Distant from our age as sin seems to have become, its correlative — guilt — strangely enough seems to abide. Guilt has two meanings. One meaning might be put in this way, that guilt is a person's eligibility for deserved punishment. That is, if the commission of a sin should bring a penalty, then guilt opens a man to the presumption that he will pay that penalty. We use guilty in this sense in the courtroom.

The second meaning of guilt, in religious terms, is derived from the expectation of punishment. In this second sense, guilt is a pervading sense or a feeling of great unworthiness — a state of the emotions which can obsess and depress a person, apart from or beyond the penalty one might expect to pay. Moreover, guilt can linger in a person as an obsession even after he has paid the requisite penalty for his trespass. Ancient Greek mythology often portrayed guilt in this sense in the form of the "Furies" who could pursue a person.

I have not fully understood the paradox that our age has virtually banished sin, but is still broadly and deeply hospitable to guilt. Perhaps we are influenced by psychoanalysis, which sets forth that the experiences of childhood linger on to shape, or

48

misshape, the adult. Mothers, who more than others influence children, can come (often mistakenly!) to feel personal guilt for the maladjustment or mental problems their adolescent or adult children experience, and the guilt-ridden mother seems to be as ubiquitous as the Jewish mother. Perhaps, though, the banishment of sin in our age has been a surface, articulate matter, but in reality the sense of sin has survived, though below the surface.

Respecting the Hebrew Bible and the New Testament, there are diverse understandings both of sin, and also of one's means for purging himself of guilt. The technical term for this latter is *atonement*. In the Hebrew Bible, sin is conceived of as an act, a discernible, external action; in the New Testament, especially in the teachings of Paul, sin is not an external action, not a single act, but rather an inner condition of man, the bondage of man to the natural, evil demands of his body; man is portrayed as possessed by the power of evil, personified by the devil. Hence, sin, as the condition of being gripped in the power of evil, is no less than the innate, normal situation of every man. This is so, because the passions of man, resident in his body, are ordinarily stronger than the restraints which the higher mind can exercise; it is the latter state of affairs that Paul reflects in his saying that, with sin resident in his body, he is unable to do what he wills to do, and he does those things that he wills not to (Romans 7:18-20). (Paul proceeds to some elaborations about the origin of sin as emerging from the Laws of Moses, but these matters need not concern us here.)

We should now turn to the matter of atonement, in view of these divergent views of sin: the Jewish view of it as a single act and the Christian view of it as the normal condition of men. In the Hebrew Bible, atonement is made by the individual himself, or by him with the help of the high priest, or even for him by the high priest, but in all these cases it is a human atonement made for one or more single, overt, external act. Moreover, the Hebrew view separates sins into two categories: the inadvertent and the deliberate. In theory, only for inadvertent sins can a man atone; if a man sins knowingly and deliberately, he is in effect

49

defying God, and there is no atonement available for deliberate sin. Indeed, where Scripture specifies particular penalties (such as the offering of an animal sacrifice) for particular trespasses, this is usually only in the case of unintentional sin; where sin, on the other hand, is deliberate, the punishment is not in human hands, but is left to God (who will "cut off" that soul from its people).

Where sin is a condition of man, as is usually the case in Paul's letters, and when man is within the power of the sin or the devil, an individual is without the capacity to purge himself; he is without the power to make his own atonement. Accordingly, in the Christian view, man does not and cannot make his own atonement; rather, atonement is viewed as having been made for man by the Christ Jesus, through his death on the cross. That is the meaning of the phrase, "Christ died for our sins." Indeed, the Jewish distinction between sin and the resultant guilt become transformed in Christian thought into the usual view that sin and guilt are simultaneous and even identical.

The effect of the Christian view is discernible in some of the derivative Christian views. Thus, sin is a natural state of man, from his very birth; a baby was expected to undergo "infant baptism" to redeem him from it. That a baby is born into sin is a consequence of guilt inherited from the ancestor of the race, Adam, who defied God in his disobedience in the garden of Eden, and this "original" sin-guilt was transmitted to his descendants. Again, in the Catholic view, Mary, the mother of Jesus, was provided with an "immaculate conception," that is, in her case, she was exempted from the guilt all other humans inherited from Adam. (Most modern people, including faithful Roman Catholics, confuse "immaculate conception" and "virgin birth"; the latter view holds that Mary had become pregnant with Jesus without human sexual intercourse; in a word, "immaculate conception" is connected with the birth of Mary, but "virgin birth" with the birth of Jesus.)

Some Protestants agree that mankind has inherited guilt from Adam, the ancestor of all; hence, the old couplet:

Yet as these Protestants have seen things, a baby undergoing baptism has this done *for* him, or *to* him, and thus that individual is deprived of the opportunity of *deciding* whether to undergo baptism or not. Such Protestants have believed that baptism necessarily has had to involve the will, and they have contended that baptism can be meaningful only when one comes to adulthood and makes a mature decision for it.

Still another derivative view, or rather set of views, has gone along the following line: Since sin is a condition natural in man, man can do nothing about it; hence there is no stake at all in whatever a man does, for he is doomed to failure. To observe the religious laws, or not to, is, moreover, irrelevant, for atonement (and, in its wake, redemption or salvation, which I discuss later) cannot be "earned." To believe that man can earn redemption by what he does is equivalent to believing that man can work his own atonement. Hence the "earning" of redemption is quite impossible. It comes, rather, as a gift; the death of the Christ Jesus on the cross was such a loving gift from God to man. ("God so loved the world that he gave his only son, so that whoever believes in him, should not perish, but should have eternal life." John 3:16)

If redemption cannot be "earned" does everyone receive this divine gift? By no means! This "free gift" is technically called *grace*. God picks out those people whom he wishes to give grace to. Such people are "elected" for redemption; indeed, there is a heavenly plan in accordance with which some people are predestined ("scheduled in advance") to receive the grace of God, and some are not. That is to say, God gives the free-gift of redemption to those whom he has decided to give it to, and withholds it from others. (This view is the consequence of holding that man cannot "earn" God's favor.)

Deeply embedded as such ideas of sin, redemption, and grace are in traditional Christianity, they have undergone both inner and external challenge. Comforting as it is to those who feel themselves elected and predestined for the grace of redemption, there is this deficit, that this view tends to negate personal moral responsibility (as we shall see a bit later). If I rob a bank because God has predestined me to do so, then God, not I, is responsible for the bank robbery. On a somewhat lower level, it is futile for a clergyman to exhort his congregants to make moral decisions as a sequel to his Sabbath preaching to them, if it is God and not man who makes the decision! Within historic Christianity, predestination was seldom carried to the point of obliterating the individual's moral responsibility or his ability to be affected by church sermonics.

But a challenge arose from Renaissance and post-Renaissance thinkers respecting this view of man's birth into sin and his inability himself to do anything about it. To such thinkers, these views seemed to degrade man. In those late medieval ages, when men began to renew the ancient sciences which the Greeks had recorded, and then moved on to develop even newer sciences, it seemed impossible to attribute to progressing man the complete disability which traditional Christianity imputed to him. The assumptions in our Declaration of Independence (derivative from Renaissance humanism) regard man as quite different from the usual Christian view of him: "We hold these views to be self-evident: that all men are created equal. That they are endowed by the Creator with certain unalienable rights, and among these rights are life, liberty, and the pursuit of happiness." Nothing is said in the Declaration of Independence of man's sinful nature, or of the inevitable failure that supposedly attends all his efforts.

Against this complex background — here presented very briefly — it perhaps becomes more readily intelligible why sin is so alien an idea today. The Christian view that sin is "natural" to man clashes with a basic "democratic" conviction that man is good; those acts which in the Hebrew view entailed sin include ancient ceremonial mandates meaningless to modern men.

Sin, then, seems to be a dead thing. It is all the more paradoxical that guilt still seems to survive.

Some modern thinkers seem prepared to equate discoveries of Freudian psychoanalysis with the Christian view, though regarding the latter as symbolic rather than literal. On the one hand, nothing seems wronger to psychologists than the phrase, "innocent as a babe," for we have now learned that even a babe has basic passions which he tries to satisfy. Moreover, man's super-ego is constantly at war with his id, and the id is in some ways kindred — so we are told — to original sin, and the super-ego to man's conscience. Furthermore, the modern person who is gripped by a sense of guilt can never (or, hardly ever) work his own way out; in place of the Christ, it is the psychoanalyst who by external guidance can lead the patient out of the grip of his guilt by bringing him to self-understanding.

It should be acknowledged that there are some strikingly similar themes as between psychiatric healing and religious redemption. Granted that this is the case, the differences are nevertheless striking, unless one is to abandon the definition of sin and to forget that its basic meaning involves trespass against God. To attribute, as I am quite ready to do, insight and effectiveness to psychoanalysis is right, but I think it rather shabby to jump to an equating of a secular medical procedure with a set of religious views.

Equally wide of the mark is still another modern effort at harmonization. This particular one properly laments the observable circumstance that many individuals in our complex society fail of self-realization; they can possess talents which never grow or flower into full achievement, or they can even fail of any achievement at all. Sin is then defined as the failure of a person to achieve self realization. Certainly we should have unlimited compassion for those who fall short of self-realization; however, to contend that such a failure is a trespass against God overlooks the very meaning of sin.

No, modern men can fall short of worthiness in a variety of ways and individually or collectively "miss the mark" — the Hebrew and Greek words for sin are basically archery terms for being wide of the target — but such failure to achieve self-realization is not quite the same as sin. Sin, if one abstains from playing with words, cannot mean anything other than failure to conform with what one believes about God and his requirements.

If one does not believe in God, one ought to desist from talking about sin.

How much personal responsibility remains when sin is dissolved and disappears? What happens to ideas of right and wrong?

IX

Man's Obligations to God

IF A BELIEF in sin is possible only if there is first a belief in God's law or will, in what way have men believed that they have learned about the latter? The answer revolves around the idea contained in the word *revelation*.

This word means "disclosure." The implied figure of speech supposes that something once lying hidden manages to come to light. We often use the words *reveal* and *revelation* in connection with human secrets, as when we say that a certain secret, or some private matter, has been revealed. Often that which is hidden is stored in a dark place, and hence when we speak about its disclosure we often say that it has "come to light."

When men believe that God is something other than a visible, tangible idol, they ordinarily also believe that God is in some sense hidden, in some way related to what is secret. Psalm 91:1 expresses this in these words:

> The Lofty One dwells in a secret place
> The Almighty lodges in the shadows.

The revelation of God means this: that though ordinarily God is hidden away, on occasion he discloses himself openly.

How? Biblical literature furnishes a variety of descriptions, for example, in the burning bush of Exodus 3:1-6, in the vivid Temple scene of Isaiah 6:1-3 (where, in God's coming to light, he is surrounded by seraphim, "fiery creatures," who proclaim, "Holy, holy, holy is the Lord of Hosts, the world is filled with his *glory*" — the real meaning of glory is "radiance"). Another term, of Greek derivation, is *theophany* — *theo* meaning God, and *phany* meaning "appearing, becoming discernible." We can say, respecting the traditions in the Hebrew Bible, that the incident recorded about Sinai is the foremost theophany in the Bible. There not only did God reveal himself, but he also proceeded to reveal his laws. Antecedent to Sinai, while God is portrayed as having revealed himself to Abraham, Isaac, and Jacob, only at Sinai is he portrayed as having revealed law and laws; indeed, the preeminence of Moses in the succession of the great men of the previous times — that is, Abraham, Isaac, and Jacob — was that to Moses God revealed his name *Yahve*, previously unknown to men, according to Exodus 3:6-15 and 6:3. The import of revealing the name is to suggest that a more complete, more encompassing revelation was made to Moses than to the three patriarchs.*

*Later ages embroidered this matter of the divine name. On the one hand, Jews concluded that the divine name must not be pronounced, some arriving at that conclusion through their interpreting "Thou shalt not take the name of the Lord thy God in vain" to be a rule against mere pronunciation; the intent in the commandment, however, was quite different, as can emerge from my paraphrase of the purpose, "If in a law-court you swear by the Lord your God, you had better tell the exact truth." A consequence of this abstention from mere pronunciation is that the name was progressively extended. The divine name was Yahve, expressed in Hebrew by the consonants YHWH; Jews, not wishing to pronounce this tetragrammaton ("four letter word"), read it *Adonoi* ("My Lord"); in medieval times, when written vowels were recorded in Bible manuscripts (before then, the writing was only consonantal), to the consonants YHWH there were added the vowels of the word Adonoi, resulting in the word *Yehowah*, appearing in its Latin form of Jehovah. In time, Jews regarded even Adonoi as pronounceable only in prayer, but never in common speech; for the latter use, *adoshem* was substituted for Adonoi; *shem* in Hebrew for name. In current publications by traditional Jews, one encounters "G-d" in place of "God," an instance of yet another extension of not pronouncing the divine name.

On the other hand, in fringes of both Jewish and Christian life, eighteen centuries ago (where religion and superstition were adjacent), the use of the name became magical, as expressed in the supposition that one could by the

Respecting the patriarchs, the Hebrew Bible speaks thus: "God appeared." The Hebrew word for appear (as is also the case in Latin and Greek) is the passive form of the verb to see; "to appear" is "to be seen." In one passage, Genesis 15, we are told that God spoke to Abraham in a "vision"; when sunset came, "a deep sleep fell on Abraham." When Jacob (Genesis 28) falls asleep and sees angels ascending and descending from a ladder stretching into heaven, God speaks to him.

Visions and dreams represent ways of the theophany in the Hebrew Bible, but more usually the theophany is expressed by a Hebrew term *galah*, "to uncover." (The same word *galah* is used for illicit human sex, for example, "to uncover the genitals" which clothing normally conceals.) A typical way of speaking is contained in a rebuking question to a man, Eli, who was ineligible for the office of priest which he held, "Did I *reveal* myself to your ancestors . . .?"

Revelation, then, means that the hidden God emerges from his place of secrecy to disclose himself. We can now modify what we said above (pages 21-22) — not only did the Hebrews discern God latently in the march of historical events, they also bequeathed a record of his theophanies to Abraham, Isaac, Jacob, climactically to Moses, and thereafter to "prophets" such as Amos, Hosea, and Isaiah.

To these men, according to biblical tradition, God spoke in clear, intelligible words. The Hebrew view goes beyond depicting God as the power that controls nations and events, and proceeds to portray him as actually speaking to man. Biblical books contain what purport to be verbtaim reports of God's words. (In the cases preeminently of Habakkuk and Jeremiah, these prophets carry on a two-way dialogue with God.)

"name of God," or by the "name of Jesus," cast out demons. The antithesis of the rigorous avoidance of the name, on the one hand, and the magical use of it, on the other, are one of several anomalies to which the Religions are host.

The Greek Jew Philo taught that God really has no name; the array of biblical terms for him were provided (so he explained) only in order that men could be able to address their prayers to the nameless God.

God's revelation of himself to Moses, according to the account in Exodus, was followed by God's speaking the Ten Commandments, and thereafter God spoke (perhaps we should say, dictated) an abundance of laws to him. If we believe that all this actually took place, we have no problem at all in knowing what the Hebrews meant by the "laws of God." Indeed, when Jews translated the Five Books of Moses into Greek, they gave them the name which still survives, *The Law*. The Hebrew term for the Five Books is Torah, "revealed teaching," a term not quite as restrictive as the word *Law*.

By *prophet*, the Hebrews meant men to whom God revealed himself and spoke in plain, intelligible words. (There will be more about this later.) By contrast, a *priest* for them was a functionary in a sanctuary, who had ways — such as casting lots (as gamblers cast dice) — of learning the divine will, but God was not conceived of as speaking in plain words to priests. (We today would term the priestly ways "magic.")

A succession of prophets (especially Amos, Hosea, Isaiah, Micah, Habakkuk, Ezekiel, and Second Isaiah) have left us a literature notable for profound insight expressed in majestic literary forms, but the historic significance of the prophets is not their profundity or literary eminence, but the belief that God truly spoke to them. They, then, in turn spoke the revealed words to the people.

The prophetic addresses derived directly from their conviction that God had, before their times, revealed his laws to the Hebrews, and, therefore, the prophets had a basis for chiding the Hebrews for their disobedience of the revealed laws. Another dimension of prophetic thought derived from an old Hebrew view that God and the Hebrews had through a "covenant,"* a contract, entered into a binding agreement obligating

*The idea of covenant as describing the terms or conditions of the relationship between God and man is central in the Hebrew Bible and appears in a very great abundance of passages, often as the key basis for the relationship. Early Christians believed, and contended, that God's covenant was no longer with the Hebrews but rather with the Christians. This covenant with Christian-

God to protect the Hebrews, and the Hebrews to be faithful to him; the cumulative breaking of God's laws had reached the point, according to the prophets, when the covenant was ruptured and annulled, and the Hebrews were bereft of God's protection. (I speak later about prophecy in the sense of prediction.)

Sin was a trespass of God's law, whether by the corporate nation or by the individual. Indeed, the covenant came to be viewed as both individual and collective; as today a man wears a button in his lapel as a sign that he belongs to the Shriners or the American Legion, or has graduated from Siwash University, so the "sign" for the Hebrews of the individual covenant with God was the circumcision performed on him on his eighth day. The Hebrew phrase is *bris-millah*, *bris* meaning covenant and *millah* meaning circumcision.

Since cumulative sin ruptured the covenant and terminated God's protection, then dire consequences such as a devastating invasion and conquest by a neighboring nation could ensue. For the Hebrew, sin necessarily led to some sequel; so did the opposite, righteousness. Sin led to punishment, righteousness to some reward.

Where there is law, there are law-courts. (Hebrew courts assembled at the city-gate, so that "city-gate" means a court.) Where there are courts, there are judges.

For sin, the supreme judge in biblical thought is God. A fascinating episode is described in Genesis 18:16-19:38. Divine messengers, having concluded their visit to Abraham (a visit in which they informed him that his sterile wife Sarah was to bear

---

ity was "new"; the covenant with the Hebrews was "old." To the books in the Hebrew Bible, Christians gave the name *Old Covenant*, and to its own books the name *New Covenant*. *Testament* today is usually used as a synonym for a person's "last will"; at one time, testament was a synonym for covenant, and hence the Christian terms *Old Testament* and *New Testament*.

Jews, unaware of, or dissenting from, the supposition that Christians have supplanted them as a party to God's covenant, ordinarily speak not of *Old Testament*, but of the *Bible*, meaning thereby what Christians mean by *Old Testament*.

him a child within a year), went on to an additional errand — to punish the wicked cities of Sodom and Gomorrah. God at that point felt that he should not conceal his intentions to destroy these evil cities from Abraham, whose conduct was the reverse of that found in the evil cities. But Abraham was aghast that God intended to destroy the cities, since conceivably some of their residents were righteous people. Abraham says to God, "You must not destroy the righteous and the wicked indiscriminately. Perhaps there are fifty righteous men there. *The Judge of all the world must not be guilty of injustice.*"

God spoke, in reply, of his willingness to spare the city for the sake of the fifty. Abraham proceeded, though, to haggle with God: suppose there were forty, or thirty, or twenty, or ten?

The story in part suggests how a holy man can intervene with God; in a later narrative, Abraham (there described as a prophet) prays successfully on behalf of a lecherous king (Genesis ch. 20).

The words italicized just above are the key words in our present discussion: "The Judge of all the world must not be guilty of injustice." The epithet of God, either in the noun Judge, or describing him in a verbal form of "to judge" is frequent in the Bible (e.g., Psalms 7:11, 50:6, 68:5, 75:7, 94:2 and elsewhere). While the Hebrews spoke of God as King or Ruler, it was God as Judge, incapable of injustice, which spurred some of their most striking profundities. God would condemn the wicked and acquit the guilty, as a human judge would. Condemnation brought punishment.

Hence, the view arose, often profoundly, that sin and righteousness had sequels. It led also to some rather superficial conclusions, for example, that righteousness automatically brought a man prosperity, long life, and abundant children, but sin automatically brought a man sickness or poverty or calamity. If one chose (notice the word, *chose*) to obey the divine law, one prospered; if one chose, though, to disobey it, one would be punished.

The Hebrews believed that man was endowed with the will and the capacity to choose: "Behold, I call heaven and earth as witnesses that I have set life and death, blessing and curse, before you; choose life, that you and your descendants may survive" (Deuteronomy 30:19). A person's prosperity or misery was a consequence of his choice of either sin or righteousness.

But what did the Hebrews observe about the experience of human beings in their time, and what do we observe in ours? Do good people prosper? Do wicked people suffer? Surely, our observations match those of the ancient Hebrews, for all of us have seen wicked people flourish, and decent people undergo disaster. How can we square our observations with the view that the supreme Judge must be free of injustice? Do not the observable prosperity of the wicked or the distress of the righteous reflect palpable divine injustice?

A term, *theodicy* (*theo*, "God"; *diky* "justice"), is used for biblical passages in which God's "true justice" is inquired into. Just as Abraham is portrayed as daring to question God, so others (Habakkuk, Second Isaiah, and the authors of Job and Fourth Ezra) also presumed to do so. Surely the God who revealed his laws should himself abide by their significance.

There is no question of theodicy possible where there is no view that God has antecedently revealed his laws and his will to man.

The Christian view of revelation entails certain difficulties both for Christians and non-Christians. These revolve around and derive from what amounts to an about-face on the matter of divine laws: Paul taught that the laws of Moses were outmoded and thereby nullified; they were no real vehicle for moving to righteousness, but, rather, an impediment. To compound this confusion, Paul argues affirmatively from the Pentateuch even while scorning the specific laws presented in it.

Not that Paul argues against standards of ethical conduct; rather, his view is that ethical conduct flows from the inspiration of the "Holy Spirit," not from the Mosaic requirements and prohibitions. The testimony of history is that after Paul's time, he became the "authority" used by libertines to justify their licentious conduct. This outcome was the consequence of

61

the inevitable vagueness and, even worse, the sheer subjectivity in his doctrine itself.

Moreover, the Sermon on the Mount is both majestic, and also productive of Christian quandaries. In form, Matthew portrays Jesus as insisting (as if against Paul) that the laws are not abolished. "Think not that I came to abolish the Law and the Prophets; I came to complete them. Not a jot or tittle is to disappear" (abridged from Matthew 5:17-20). There then follow seven matters which in form are meant to suggest that the particular stipulations in the laws of Moses were too lax and needed to be replaced by the increased severity of the new laws which Jesus was teaching. Thus, the prohibition of murder is increased to a prohibition of murderous thoughts, and the prohibition of adultery increased to a prohibition of adulterous thoughts, and Jewish safeguards respecting divorce give way to its complete prohibition:* "Keep your oaths" now becomes "never take an oath"; equal justice ("an eye for an eye") becomes an injunction to abstain from resisting evil, "turn the other cheek."

Is such "legislation" viable? Can a court of law deal with murderous thoughts or adulterous wishes? What can Christians possibly mean when they speak of God's laws (as Senator Sam Ervin has repeatedly done in his chairmanship of the Senate Watergate Committee)? The quantity of Protestant theological literature which scorns Judaism for its bondage to a "dry and arid legalism" is a reflection not alone of arrogance, but of a Christian wish to have it both ways — to speak of "divine laws" and at the same time to scorn the Old Testament presentation of them.†

One who takes the trouble to read Protestant writers and observes their struggles in trying to harmonize such diverse mat-

---

*In Matthew 5:32, divorce is possible on grounds of adultery, but Mark, Luke and Paul prescribe a total prohibition.

†Having first followed the lead of Paul in abrogating the Mosaic laws, the Catholic Church thereafter proceeded to develop its mammoth Canon Law, which Protestants, in their turn, have rejected.

ters as the sanctity of the Old Testament, the disparagement by Paul of Mosaic laws, the eminence of the Sermon on the Mount, and the Epistle of James (which brings "works" back into Christianity as a real force by the rear door — and called forth the wrath of Martin Luther) is caught between sympathy for Christian earnestness and — to be frank — astonishment at still another example of how elastic religious minds can be. The confusion of Christians is a source of distress to them that can be documented; to non-Christians, the Christian attitudes are so diverse and contradictory as to constitute a veritable labyrinth, a maze out of which their leaders seem unable to guide insiders or external observers.

This is the case because Christians have renounced the bill of particulars about sin as acts, in favor of a largely vague notion about it as an innate condition of man. And, thereafter, the social evils of poverty and rightlessness of poor whites and of blacks has gone unprotested by some Christians (or even defended by some), while such "evils" as drinking, gambling, and dancing have not. It is hard to imagine a more flagrant trivialization of religion.

The issues are not much different in depth for modern traditional Jews. Central in the Mosaic laws are requirements for the offering of animal sacrifices at the Temple in Jersualem; that Temple was destroyed in A.D. 70 and thereafter it became the viewpoint that *temporarily*, until the Temple will have been rebuilt, prayer is an adequate substitute for sacrifice. Traditional Jews continue to study about these sacrifices prescribed in the ancient biblical legislation and to create ever new elucidations about them in new, learned commentaries.

The enfranchisement of prayer in place of sacrifice among Jews has lasted now for almost 1900 years, yet traditional Jews still pray for the rebuilding of the Temple and the renewal of the sacrificial cult. It ought to be said, though, that I know not even one Jew of whatever stripe — ultra-traditional or radical — who cares a tinker's dam about rebuilding the Jerusalem Temple and renewing the animal sacrifice.

Not only the sacrificial laws, but also the array of what we would call civil laws — business contracts and the sale of property, for example — that are an inherent part of the totality of rabbinic laws have fallen into disuse, for most Jews do not just ignore them but are even unaware of their existence. In the area of pietistic practices (here meant as the opposite of civil law about theft or burglary), a Jew is forbidden to provide heat or light in his house on the Sabbath on the supposition that work is involved even today in flicking an electric switch. A Jew may move to a suburb and then have to stay away from synagogue worship where the walking distance is great, for he is forbidden to ride on the Sabbath. The quantity of Jewish laws was very great, for a natural cumulative tendency was operative, and biblical laws were expanded into early rabbinic law, and the latter further expanded into an even greater quantity of later rabbinic law. I have said the laws have fallen into disuse; they have never been, as it were, "repealed." In traditional Judaism, outworn laws cannot be repealed, for the traditional laws are deemed eternal, and while the inherited laws could be added to, they could not be subtracted from, since in Judaism no person or assembly of persons is or has been authorized to repeal laws. The *cul de sac* is a striking one in that palpably reduction and modification have long been realistically needed, but these are "illegal." (Reform Judaism took the iconoclastic step of "repealing" in the form of declaring the rabbinic laws to be obsolete, but Reform said almost nothing about biblical laws, as if to imply these were still valid.) Let me give one single example of the dilemma. Biblical law permits a man to divorce his wife; rabbinic law made it more specific that the privilege of divorce was restricted to men and was not available to women. In the early 1900s, when persecution in Eastern Europe spurred emigration to the western hemisphere, there were women who found themselves completely abandoned by their disloyal, emigrating husbands. If such a woman were in time to be courted by some other man, she could not qualify for eligibility for second marriage as a widow without clear proof of her husband's death, nor was she permitted to initiate a divorce; there was absolutely nothing such a deserted wife could do. Rabbinic leaders could do no more than cluck sympathetically and lament that the laws were subject neither to repeal nor even to what would amount to an implied reduction. The options open to a person caught in such a dilemma were to abide by the law and be frustrated, or else simply to ignore the whole business, as, for example, by getting a divorce through a secular civil court in place of a desired religious one. That God had ordained that a deserted wife should have absolutely no redress within Judaism was calculated only to lead those people adversely affected directly, or their sympathetic associates, to a denial that such laws were divine.

Modern people, whether of Christian or Jewish background, then, face the quandary of not truly knowing what in their traditions are reliable, on-going definitions of sin. They know intuitively that sin is something wrong and seem ready to accept the notion that some things are right and some wrong, but they fall short of an easy, precise comprehension. Thereafter, they become selective, attributing the right to what they subjectively like and the wrong to what they subjectively disapprove of. Yet they would deny that they repudiate sin, and would do so earnestly.

There is no easy way out of the quandary. One begins to understand sin only when one clarifies for oneself what one believes about God, and what one believes that God expects from man. In a general sense, sin is acting out of conformity with what one believes God expects. If one can readily conform with what is taught in a Religion, the way is somewhat easier; if one cannot do so readily, the way is arduous.

X

Salvation-Redemption: God's Obligation to Man

IN THE JEWISH-CHRISTIAN tradition, the relation between God and man was expressed, as we have said, in a covenant. Each of the contracting parties was viewed as having specific responsibilities, man to obey and worship God, and God to guide and protect man.

The day-to-day events we go through have often seemed (and can still seem) to have no direct bearing on God-and-man relations. But there can be acute situations which arise. Such is the case in extreme dangers (when a ship seems on the verge of sinking, or a military invasion threatens the safety and, indeed, the lives of people). Frequently, a feeling of despair, a lack of hope, accompanies some specific danger.

Despair, however, may more often be chronic; a person is gripped by it when an incurable illness comes into the family or when an array of problems — financial or occupational — seem beyond human solution. Moreover, there are those people whose moods are pessimistic, viewing life as completely futile, with the inevitability of death underscoring that futility. In such varying situations of despair, men have looked to God for reassurance or even help.

The terms *salvation* and *redemption* are synonyms. The supposition behind the terms is that man is in a perilous situation, and that it is God's obligation in respect to the covenant to save him from the peril. Christians attribute the saving to the Christ, God's "representative," and hence they address Jesus as

"Savior." The Hebrew Bible, in a good many passages, speaks of God himself as having saved his people; the enslavement from Egypt is by far the best-known event in the Hebrew Bible when God "saved" his people.

The Christian view adds something not found in the Hebrew Bible. There, God *in this world* rescues man from his danger. Since the Hebrew Bible is a legacy which became part of Christendom, that view is found in Christendom also. The added element, however, is the Christian view that salvation has to do with the power of sin and of death — not death as a blow from a human enemy but rather death as the destiny of every man; that is, God saves man *from this world* in which death is inevitable. To put this in another way, in the Hebrew Bible salvation is God's rescue from an external danger, brought on by a circumstance such as some powerful foe; the added Christian element deals not with external danger, but with man's completely inner despair, this stemming from his innate condition as a sinner (the consequence of which is death, and hence the phrase, "the wages of sin are death"). The death of Jesus on the cross is viewed as having brought mankind release from sin and hence from the destiny of man's dying.

The Christian sects differ in whether they take "salvation" literally or only figuratively. The view of salvation as eliminating death seems to be a change from a previous notion, "resurrection." The change seems a product of Christianity's becoming at home in the Greek world, where resurrection was unknown, but salvation, that is, escape from man's innate condition and from death, was found in the Greek mystery religions and, indeed, was their basic purpose.

The main lines of Jewish thought have lacked this Christian view of salvation in the sense of escape. Hence, a frequent contrast is made: Judaism is described as a religion "of this world," and Christianity as "otherworldly." What is wrong with this contrast is that it is only a partial truth, in that in domains other than salvation, Judaism has been notably otherworldly, and Christianity has had a social concern that has been extremely "this worldly" (exemplified by its hospitals, orphanages, and philanthropic institutions). Partisans argue (vainly, but eloquently!) as to which of the two systems is superior or the more realistic. Surely it is more important to notice the reality of the overlaps — that in both traditions God is viewed as able to redeem his people from danger — and to be attentive to the additional view of Christians that God saves man from this world. Yet is there not a danger that the belief in God's salvation can seem to some people a justification for human inactivity, for spiritual laziness, for shirking the duties that men ought to respond to?

That God rescues man from a danger, or an illness, or an intolerable problem often entails a belief in a "miracle." In its ordinary sense, a miracle is a suspension of the usual workings of cause and effect, such as the account of the sun's standing still in Joshua 10:12-13, Elisha's making an iron axe float in the water (2 Kings 6:1-6), or Jesus' walking on the water (Matthew 14:25). Because the working of nature as we understand it is ruptured by a miracle, we speak of miracles as being *supernatural*, "above nature." Miracles occur, so the Religions hold, when God personally intervenes to suspend the usual working of nature.

Scripture has a multitude of accounts of miracles, these a reflection of the environment of ancient times when miracles did not spur the disbelief which is characteristic of our age. In the Religions, there is a recurrent view that somehow or other the age of miracles is now past, probably because of man's hardheartedness, but the accounts of the ancient biblical miracles are viewed as quite credible.

There are some interpreters who handle biblical miracles shabbily, this by eliminating the supernatural element so as to retain the historical; for example, one scholar "explained" Jesus' walking on the water as an error on the part of his disciples who did not see the sand bar on which Jesus was walking. Surely it is more honest to disbelieve in biblical miracles than to rob them of the supernatural element in order to make them credible.

It has become quite usual in our time for the word *miracle* to lack a supernatural aspect; we use the term today to mean something wonderful, yet quite natural. We speak of "miracle" drugs, and some manufacturers of soap detergents or of washing machines advertise them as performing "miracles." The use of miracle in this sense robs the word of its import in the religious meaning of the term.

It is not hard to understand that people, harassed by acute problems of deep dimension, turn to God for help when all else seems to fail. One should, so it seems to me, have boundless sympathy for such people, and one ought not try to deter them from their urgent need to call on God. But good minds in the Religions seem right in asserting that there are those who seem to think that they can, in an almost superstitious way, coerce God into a supernatural intervention, by praying for it or by demanding it. The best minds have counselled against such expectations. These expectations have arisen, in part, because of passages in Scripture which in their plain sense do assure the faithful that God responds at the call of man: "Ask, and you will receive; search, and you will find; knock, and the door will be opened" (Matthew 7:7). The full record of man's past would disclose a multitude of instances when a welcome miracle simply did not ensue at someone's request. For a person to rely on convenient, gratifying miracles is to give way to sanctioned foolhardiness.

Salvation in the sense of God's interruption of the working of nature to rescue a person or a people can seem to some people credible but to others incredible. We respond about such things, as in other facets of religion, in the light of our dispositions and our needs. We can neither prove nor disprove the statement that miracles occur or the statement that they do not. Not to believe in miracles emphasizes man's helplessness and loneliness. To believe in them can raise the risk of being deluded. There is, though, an even greater risk in the matter of expecting easy miracles, namely, the danger of trivializing either man or God, or both.

XI

Theodicy: Is God Just?

IF MEN ACCEPT the premise that God is the Judge of perfect justice, how have they dealt with the injustices in society that become evident to an honest observer? By assumption, injustice is an evil. If a nation, or an individual, undergoes undeserved evil, then the thinking person comes to question God's justice.

One way of dealing with the problem, found in the Bible, was to challenge the validity of the human perception, this by suggesting that what in the short range appears to man to be an evil can in the long range turn out to be good. A form of this is the point of the biblical account of Joseph. Out of jealousy, his brothers sold him into slavery. He rose to the second highest position in Egypt as a result of his insight in storing food in years of plenty against coming years of famine. He provided food for his family — the plot is complex — and then became reunited with them. After the father's death, the brothers, fearing Joseph's vengeance for what they had done to him, sought his mercy, and even offered to become his slaves. He replied: "Am I in God's place? You devised evil against me; God intended it for good, to preserve life, as has happened."

In normal human experience, it often happens that what at first seems an evil turns out not to be so. A person, losing a coveted job, turns to something else and achieves a fantastic, unlooked-for success, which could not have come about had he not lost the coveted job. Well enough! But not every evil turns into a good, and one does not really comprehend evil by depriving it of its genuine meaning, as happens when evil is viewed as a hidden, disguised good.

70

A second biblical way of handling the problem was to suppose that some good outcome can counterbalance a truly evil experience. The Book of Job has an ending tacked on to it that tells that after Job's ordeal of the undeserved loss of his family, position, and wealth, he emerged with new wealth replacing his lost fortune, and new children replacing those he had been bereaved of. One wonders how deeply the author of the tacked-on ending probed the suffering on Job's part at the point when he lost his children! Moreover, in ordinary experience, not every one who undergoes distress is fortunate enough to move on thereafter to a turn in affairs supposedly able to compensate him.

One more ancient way of dealing with the question of theodicy was to suppose that God brought suffering to man in order to chasten and refine him. I imagine that all of us have known people who, in our estimation, have risen from little character to some, or from some to a great deal, as a consequence of misfortune and unexpected responsibility; I think we would not want to deny the reality of the chastening effect of misfortune. But suppose misfortune comes, and its effect is not to chasten and refine a person but to produce in him unrelieved bitterness and acute self-pity? The ancient rabbis left the dictum that if afflictions come upon a man, he should first seek to understand them as a result of his misconduct. If, though, he is satisfied that his own misconduct does not adequately explain his afflictions, he should next seek to know if he has neglected the requisite study of the holy books. If he is satisfied that he has not neglected the requisite study, he can conclude that he has undergone "afflictions of love" — a phrase that comes from Proverbs 3:12 — to the effect that God chastens those whom he loves, as a father the son he delights in. But endless affliction is scarcely an adequate price to pay for divine love, as is attested to by an ancient rabbi; he said that he was content to do without the love if thereby he could avoid the afflictions! To attribute afflictions to God's love can be little other than one more admission that we do not understand the why of evil.

To turn to another effort to understand the why of evil, the poem in the Book of Job (that is, the poem as distinct from the prose prologue and epilogue) is the most profound inquiry into theodicy ever written. Job has undergone supreme disaster in the abrupt loss of his wealth, his personal eminence, his children, and his good health. He seeks to understand how a just God could have let this happen, or indeed, could have arranged for this to happen. His speeches — masterly poems — inquire into the elusive why of it all, and Job's inquiry is punctuated by the speeches of three visitors who seem to have all the answers to all questions. Their collective answer is a very simple one: God is just; as righteousness leads to divine reward, so sin leads to distressing punishment; hence, Job's calamities are his punishment for what must have been a record of antecedent sins. Job's visitors, by so reasoning, have no problem in understanding evil.

Job's difficulty is occasioned by his certainty of his past innocence. Had he truly been a sinner in the past, he would have had no problem (and we would not have inherited this remarkable book). Because he had not been a sinner, but rather a righteous man, he sought, profoundly and desperately, to come to an understanding of the ways of God. With the fullest measure of poetic eloquence, he maintains his innocence of sin, both to his three visitors and to God, and he courageously withstands the efforts of the former to prove him a past sinner. The climax of the book is for some readers a disappointment: God, appearing to Job in a whirlwind, informs Job that man simply does not possess the wisdom to understand such ultimate questions of why.

In the biblical allusions above, the assumption has been made that evil comes from God, for it is he who controls the march of events. One more ancient way out of the problem of theodicy was to deny that God could be the source of evil. Apparently the Persians had explained evil by supposing that two forces exist in the world, the good God and the evil one. Biblical monotheism could not go this way; instead, the view arose that within God's rule there was a separate source of, or force for, evil, called *Satan* in Hebrew. The word in origin means "shadow." Our word *devil* is an English variation of the Greek translation for the Hebrew Satan.

It is possible from surviving literature to see how the views about the devil grew in dimension in the centuries after its first appearance in the Bible. He is presented first as an underling of God; in later writings he emerges as a rebellious rival who comes to exercise sovereignty over the earth* and finally becomes the autocrat of hell, the place to which the dead go. The devil is in a sense an idea or a device to solve the problem of theodicy, by imputing evil to him rather than to God himself. The prose prologue to Job "explains" the sufferings of Job as due to Satan, to whom God gives consent to test Job as to whether or not his sufferings will destroy his belief in God. (Thus the prologue and the later poem differ from each other in two ways: the prologue, ascribing evil to Satan, makes Job a man exposed to a cruel test, while the poem, ascribing evil to God, makes Job the exemplar of all innocent men whose sufferings are quite other than a mere test and part of the normal experience of many.)

Yet another solution for the problem of theodicy was sought for in the Jewish (and then the Christian) view of the afterlife. Involved was a view of two eras of time — the one this dismal age (the here and now) and the other a future world destined to come some day. In most Jewish thought, the world to come was conceived of as belonging to the very remote future, but periodically there arose those who expressed the conviction that the world to come was near at hand (this is the case, for example, with Paul). After sufficient predictions of the early arrival of the new age resulted in the disappointing recognition that it still had not come, the notion of futurity was modified (not abandoned!) by the supposition that the age to come was already

---

*In the Gospels, it is a presupposition that the earth has come under the sovereignty of the devil. The phrase "Thy kingdom come" is a prayer that God, rather than the devil, should rule the earth. Jesus is portrayed as first resisting the devil, and then of besting him, thereby ushering in the kingdom of God.

available in the present, with admission into it gained through death. One could go, as it were, into the world to come by dying, rather than by waiting for the unknown and remote future to roll around. As this relates to theodicy, the view arose that the injustices conceded to exist in the here and now would be straightened out in the world to come, this by rewards there meted out to the righteous, and punishment inflicted on the wicked. A differentiation came into being, that the righteous for their reward went to "heaven," and the wicked for their punishment went to "hell," where the devil had come to reign.

Had the author of Job written later than in the unknown age when he lived (probably about 500-400 B.C.), he could have offered as a solution for Job's acute distress the expectation that the injustice done to him would be redressed in the afterlife. The Book of Job was written before the Hebrews broadly accepted a belief in an afterlife. It was quite some time later (about three centuries) that theodicy underwent the solution of supposing that God's justice is only being delayed, and its appearance is certain to arrive in the afterlife.

Heaven and hell underwent considerable embellishment in the late Old Testament period. Thus, seven different Hebrew words for what is above the clouds led to the view that there were seven layers of heaven. One recalls the song from Show Boat, "Why Do I Love You?":

> I'm in the seventh heaven,
> They're more than seven!. . .

Not only were the injustices of this world rectified in heaven by rewards to the righteous, but poverty and hunger in this life would there be counterbalanced by wealth and feasting. The sex-starved man could envisage there a host of beauteous and available women! Indeed, the Jewish and Christian traditions present forthright denials of some of the "coarse" expectations of what heaven was to provide simply because there were those who had such expectations.

74

Christians embellished the concept hell beyond their inheritance of the idea from Judaism, this to the point that some modern Jews, disbelieving in hell, incorrectly assert it never existed in Judaism. In the Catholic tradition, *limbo* ("edge" or "border") is a place bordering on hell; to it there went (only for a period of delay) the souls of those just people who died before the time of Christ, and also (though forever) the souls of those innocent people, later than Christ, who died without proper baptism, being thus barred from entering heaven. Heaven for Christians is the abode of the clearly redeemed; there they live with angels. Hell is the abode to which the clearly wicked go for their punishment.

If one believes in an afterlife where reward or punishment awaits one, the problem of theodicy is solved. Without such a belief, however, the problem lingers on unsolved. One rather recent effort to solve this problem has been to deny either that God existed or still exists ("God is dead" or "God died at Auschwitz"). This is a reversal of the old biblical effort; in the Bible there were those who "explained" evil by denying in effect that there was such. If one denies that God exists, then he has no need to explain evil, for he has no reason to try to reconcile a nonexistent God of justice with the reality of evil.

Men, whether ordinary men or philosophers, cannot reasonably solve the problem of theodicy. An individual may, if he wishes, embrace one of the above views, or else some personal modification of it, consistent with his personal bent. We do not solve the problem of evil by *knowledge*; at best we adjust to evil in terms of whatever we come to believe. But there is a bit more to say.

All too often we are influenced in childhood by a motif in the fairy tales "and they lived happily ever after" into supposing that living happily ever after potentially awaits all of us. We all yearn for a "summertime when the living is easy." We tend to think and act as if evil has no proper place in our lives, that evil, if it comes, is something that intrudes — and really has no business intruding. Evil seems capable of astonishing us by appearing in our experience without our preparation for it. The reality, however, is that despite whatever ease we periodically achieve, living is arduous, and living happily ever after, with no rupture of pure bliss, is a condition denied us. We may at times be able to transcend our disappointments and achieve some satisfaction in the necessary substitute for our preferred pursuits and goals; we may even have the inner strength to survive veritable calamities. But disappointments, and a diversion to substitute goals, are the experience of even the most fortunate of us, and none of us is immune to the possibility of tragedy or the accompanying sorrow and even despair; this is the truth about living. The ancient rabbis, so it is reported, engaged in a debate on whether it was better to be born or not born; rather quaintly, they even took a vote on the issue, and the count showed that it was better not to have been born! Perhaps that is excessive negativism, but it is surely a worthy counterbalance to the insipid notion that life is, or can be, an unbroken joy. We ought, moreover, to tell the children we bring into the world the truth about what can lie ahead, instead of happy fairy tales.

Perhaps our ability to be "surprised" by evil arises from the acute displeasure of the weaknesses that turn up in our friends and associates who prove unworthy of our confidence in them. An unlooked-for personal betrayal, an act of infidelity, or an unexpected (and undeserved) hostility or animosity can take us unawares. We tend, though, to regard these as exceptional, as against the very tenor of our reasonable expectations.

Quite beyond what persons do to us (for people are prone to do bad or nasty things), it is reasonable for us to live in the knowledge that sickness, distress, bereavement, or sheer calamity can overtake us, sometimes without any advance warning. Insurance policies, in the fine print, speak of exemptions available to the insuring companies through what they still call "acts of God"; what they mean is that no human culprit is to be found, and that the company is not culpable.

Automobiles do collide, and planes do fall; ladders do topple, and fires do break out; illnesses — sharp and acute, or slow and lingering — are not rare occurrences. Violence, revolution, and war are recurrent in society. For most of us, these misadventures, if they occur, come at scattered intervals, with so little frequency that we experience long intervals of being at ease, so that we can ordinarily lead our lives with little or no awareness of the reality of evil. Only a fraction of us experience starkest tragedy; all of us, though, experience losses and grief.

What are we to do when these come? Certainly we are entitled to grieve. Certainly we ought not try to restrain the tears (as if such restraint implies commendable strength). Certainly we ought to push ourselves into understanding how the tragedy and our personal religious beliefs can align themselves.

What we should not do is respond as if a misfortune completely without historical precedent has come uniquely to us and that we are experiencing what no one in the history of the human race has experienced. Alas, this latter is not true.

Moreover, to protract our grief, to extend it unreasonably, is harmful to us. It is the part of wisdom (and a healing of the inner person) for us to rise above the misfortune of the moment and return to our usual obligations and routines.

If we cannot understand the why of the evils that befall man, and therefore befall us too, we can at least understand the universal character of what men undergo.

XII

Rewards and Punishment

THE RELIGIONS BEQUEATH to us contradictory injunctions. They tell us, on the one hand, that either reward or punishment can await us as a consequence of our deeds; they also tell us that to obey and serve God deliberately as the means of qualifying for a reward represents a low motive which debases religion. I should imagine that, on the articulate level, most of us would subscribe to the notion that when the motive of a person for some action is to escape punishment or to earn a reward, then that conscious motive is not as exalted as it is to practice virtue for its own sake. Nevertheless, most of us are so reared as to be tightly caught in the net of rewards and punishment.

It is a very ancient net. In the realm of secular law we have not as yet fully extricated ourselves from it respecting legal punishment. However much our penal systems have progressed beyond incarcerating a man's family with him in a debtor's prison or locking up even a harmless insane person in a public jail, we still live in systems in which there is a supposition, or at least a hope, that the punishment fits the crime, with the result that gradations in terms of imprisonment or in the amount of fines abide among us. Unconsciously we continue to carry this array of the quid pro quo into our normal religious thinking: punishment conforms to the quantity of our sin, and reward to the quantity of our righteousness.

The playwright Ibsen in *Ghosts* illustrated an idea found in the Bible, in the words ascribed to God, that he visits the sins of the fathers on children or grandchildren, even to the fourth generation (Exodus 34:7). Ibsen's example of this was the transmission of venereal disease to an unborn child.

If our thinking is clear, we can differentiate between our observation that families are indeed prone to suffer for the misdeeds of one of its members; surely it happens. This, though, is quite different from supposing that worthy descendants of an evil man should bear some inherited guilt from the evil ancestor. Most of us would conclude, so I think, that children can inherit shame (as do young Germans), but they ought not bear guilt (as their Nazi forbears should). The idea of the transfer of guilt is a horrendous one, by any standard; it is rejected in the Bible itself in the words of two prophets, Jeremiah and Ezekiel. They quote a proverb, "The fathers have eaten sour grapes, so that the teeth of the children are set on edge." They quote the proverb, accompanied by their assertion that it ought never be spoken again. Both assert, rather, that each person bears responsibility only for his own actions, not for what father or grandfather did.

When a family, as happens, suffers from the misdeeds of a member, this is simply a case of the proverbial bystander who, though innocent, undergoes injury or damage. That the family of certain individuals does undergo damage as bystanders is an unhappy reality. But we ought not to cite the passage from Exodus of God's punishing children for their grandparents' sins as if it is the sole biblical viewpoint — and as if the injured deserved what they got! In light of the prophetic rejection of the proverb about sour grapes, the belief that God punishes grandchildren seems to be a traditional, old view that the courageous Jeremiah and Ezekiel dared to contradict and to combat.

If we follow the lead of Jeremiah and Ezekiel, of necessity we will look on all peoples as individuals, representing neither families, nor nations, nor religions. The religious person can have no justification for racial, religious, or national bias.

XIII

Birth, Marriage, Death

FAR AS PEOPLE may stray from the Religions, marriage ceremonies and funeral rites still seem to remain occasions when people turn to the clergy. Granted that a few couples seek out a judge or justice of the peace to marry them, and occasional funerals take place without a clergyman, there is something about the milestones of life that impels a person toward the Religions, even in our unsettled times.

This is so in part because of a heritage — though seldom on the articulate level — that the milestone events of birth, marriage, and death are so intimately connected with the mystery of living that on these occasions even people estranged from the Religions turn to them.

It was suggested earlier that even though we fully understand the physiology of sexual intercourse, we can nevertheless feel awe that from it new humans are born. The awe arises from the seeming disconnection between mere semen and a new life. Again, the nine months of pregnancy, even with our advanced medicine, still provide the uncertainty: Will it eventuate in a whole baby, without blemish, born in normal manner, with the mother's generously given pain, or will it result in a stillborn infant or one born pathetically maimed in body or mind? Will the mother pass through the travail without that prospect of disaster that existed a century ago when so many women died in childbirth? Awe at a new life and anxiety for baby and mother are ancient, so very ancient as to defy any effort to trace the earliest records of them. It is no accident that the Bible increases

80

the wonder of childbearing by telling us that great women, Sarah, Rebekah, and Hannah were initially sterile, for their conceiving was viewed as no less than miraculous. It is no accident that a wondrous birth was ascribed to Isaac, in that, as we are told specifically, Sarah was beyond the age of fertility (Genesis 18:11) and Abraham was a very old man. It is no accident that, in a different, later environment, the birth of Jesus is narrated as having been unreservedly miraculous, the child of a virgin who had not known a man. The special miracles emphasize how miraculous even ordinary conception and birth were deemed.

Religious rites have naturally clustered about childbirth. One of these, circumcision, is often explained as giving to the deity the foreskin of the generative organ, both in thanks that the child was born, and to preserve his life so that in time he too can generate. Baptism of a baby in Christianity preserves him for the future; a relic of Catholic baptism, recently featured in a movie, is the rite of the exorcism of demons. It probably seems strange to us that in the Hebrew Bible, a mother through bearing a child is thereby rendered ritually "impure"; we cannot be sure of the reason for this, but it appears to go along this line: that in bearing the child, the mother has trespassed into the divine realm, and such trespass is fraught with danger unless she frees herself from it by going through rites of purification. A man who, asleep at night, has an emission of semen is likewise rendered impure. Rabbinic tradition tells that a stand-by was appointed for the High Priest in preparation for the rites of the Day of Atonement, lest a nocturnal emission render him impure and disqualify him from officiating.

For our purposes, we shall define puberty as the stage a boy or girl reaches when he or she becomes capable of parenthood. The external signs are the growth of pubic hair, the boy's ability to discharge semen, and the girl's experience of menstruation. Our legacy of Puritanism (both Christian and Jewish) have concealed aspects of the older responses to the wonder of puberty. Among Jews, *bar mitzvah* (defined in the tradition as entering

81

into grown-up responsibility for the Jewish laws) was set at the age of thirteen because at the time it was innovated (about the year 1000 B.C.) male puberty arrived at about that age. Menstruation was deemed (like childbirth) to defile a woman; an orthodox rabbi will not shake hands with a woman lest he acquire her impurity. The piquant "handkerchief dance" in *Fiddler on the Roof*, in which the rabbi participated, was a device to avoid contamination by the direct touch of a possibly "impure" person. The total quantity of folk traditions relating to puberty are beyond summarizing here.

The mystery of sexual procreation is reflected in two opposite developments. One is the exaltation of virginity. Promiscuity on the part of a girl who became pregnant obscured the identity of the father, who would be obligated for support of mother and child. (In traditional Judaism, the definition of whether a person is Jewish or not depends on the person's mother; if she is Jewish, the child is too; if the mother is Gentile and the father Jewish, the child is not deemed Jewish. Why? Because people can know for certain who the mother is, but not who the father is.) A priest was permitted by biblical law to marry only a virgin; a widow or a divorcee were forbidden him. Long, long before Victorian times, virginity had become a young woman's most precious possession, an accepted symbol of her wholeness and purity. In some ancient religions, priestesses of the goddesses, especially of "chaste Diana" preserved their virginity throughout their lives (as do Catholic and Anglican nuns today). Yet at another extreme, in ancient agricultural religions, temples were peopled with sacred prostitutes; a male worshiper, by having socially approved intercourse with a sacred prostitute on a holy day, was "imitating" the union of the sun and the earth, thereby promoting the sun's impregnation of the earth so that it becomes Mother Earth. (Again the abundance of related folklore is beyond summary here.)

The sense of possession (*my* wife, *her* husband) which arises in marriage (a relic of the time when the man literally owned the wife) could be violated by adultery. For that reason, it was deemed illicit to have sexual relations with other than one's spouse. And just as a man wanted to preserve the gratification of his ego through the sexual fidelity of the woman he had married, he transferred that demand onto the girl he planned or hoped to marry. A girl not a virgin was deemed to be prone to adulterous infidelity; hence, the supposition was that a girl who was virgin before her marriage would be a model of fidelity after it. Of course men and women "cheat"; most modern people are unaware of a section of Scripture (Numbers 5:11-22) which deals with the "trial by ordeal" a wife could be forced to go through if her husband suspected her of an act of infidelity. An important plot incident in the novelette about Joseph is the effort of Potiphar's wife to lure her husband's servant Joseph into her bed. Hence, the best but uncertain insurance a man could have against a faithless wife was to pick a girl who at betrothal was a virgin.

In the Catholic tradition, Mary was not only a virgin at the birth of Jesus, but remained one forever; the "sisters and brothers" mentioned in Mark 6:3 are interpreted by Catholics as cousins.

Why, to repeat, was there such a premium placed on virginity? Because its termination could result in the creation of a new life, with the act of procreation seeming in some way to partake of God's creative power.

By some quirk of anatomy, a girl is born with a hymen, "a maidenhead," which initial intercourse ruptures, and some bleeding ordinarily results. In the ancient world, blood on the bedclothes immediately after the first night could attest to the virginity of the bride. Perhaps the male's lack of a physical counterpart accounts for the absence from ancient languages of a male counterpart to the word *virgin*.

The rupture of the hymen in the sex act results from its being punctured by the male organ in its aroused, erect form. As men grow old, erection occurs less frequently, and intercourse can become impossible. Somewhat similarly, among younger men disturbances (probably psychic in origin) can impede the requisite erection. The male inability to perform we term *impotence* ("absence of strength"). Impotence in itself would be mystery enough; the relationship of potency and impotence to procreation increased the aura of the mystery. Men, eager for potency, have often sought for medications or special diets to assure it. There is available for the curious an abundance of folklore — ranging from a recourse to oysters, through aphrodisiacs, through "monkey glands" — about potency.

In the primitive religions, the desired potency was expressed visually in symbols — such as straight up and down stones or the maypole — representing the erect male organ. When the organ is erect, it is called a *phallus*; unaltered, it is simply the *penis* ("that which hangs"). A phallic symbol could, on the one hand, assure a man that his organ would not fail him, or on the other hand, it could express man's wonder at the power in this organ to beget a new life.

The basic objection of the Hebrews to the adoration of the phallus as in Canaanite religion was the inherent suggestion that it itself rather than God was the agent of procreation. Hence, biblical literature scorns and disparages the Canaanite religion where, so we may put it, the sex organs became the object of adoration in place of God. The misuse of the organs, as in homosexuality, was forbidden; prostitution was forbidden. Masturbation* is not mentioned but "onanism" is, this in a narrative. The man Onan was obligated to marry the childless widow of his brother; he withdrew prior to orgasm, spilling his seed on the ground, and for this trespass (so runs the account) the Lord slew him.

That the sex act can involve procreation gave it a sense of re-

---

*When marriage took place (as once it did) at or near puberty, rather than after a delay of at least a decade (as in our society), there was no need for a period such as that which the Victorian age tacitly approved of — "sowing wild oats"; fornication (illicit sex relations between the unmarried) was then not needed. Indeed, the tight controls that existed over girls reduced the opportunity for fornication.

84

ationship to God's domain of creation. Moreover, in ancient society where legacies were to be bequeathed, the birth of a son and heir was a concern to the families of bride and groom, not just the personal preoccupation of the couple. The personal element of love between groom and bride, so dominant in modern marriage, scarcely existed; rather, marriages united family lines.* If by chance a man married a shrew, he could proceed to divorce her, but such a divorce was an extremity that, though available, ought not to be called on. Polygamy was possible, but it was expensive and beyond the capacity of the usual man; under polygamy a man could escape the discomforts of a shrew by turning elsewhere in his household, without needing to leave home.

That a marriage could result in either joy or distress was naturally evident to any observer. A biblical verse was twisted slightly by the ancient rabbis so as to yield a point, namely, that a meritorious man won a "helpmate," but a man devoid of merit won an "antagonist." The uncertainty of the outcome of a marriage was underscored by a quaint rabbinic story which conceived of God as the great matchmaker who, once he had completed the creation of the world, turned to deciding who should marry whom. It was told that a Roman emperor, hearing of this Jewish crotchet, scorned the notion that marriages were made in heaven and thought that he could do better than the Jewish God. The emperor's harvest of his effort was an endless number of couples who were injured, crippled, maimed — and he concluded that the notion that marriages were made in heaven was quite admirable.

The ideas which have been dominant in the last two centuries, that marriage is a matter of personal fulfillment, and, indeed,

---

*Vestiges in abundance abide, not only in royal marriages, but in the continuing custom by which the parents of the bride, not the bride herself, issue the invitations to a wedding. What has now virtually disappeared, though, is the practice of a direct, overt financial settlement by the parents, along with the medieval custom of haggling over the dowries.

the private business of a couple questing for a satisfying romance, represent a drastic turnabout. The constantly growing divorce rate in the western world is its own commentary on the progression involved from the medieval "business marriage" to the modern "self-fulfilling" one.

One must go on to say that the sexual aspect in the premodern forms of marriage were so taken for granted as to seem to have been relatively free of the modern recurrent neuroses of impotence and frigidity; these appear to be products of romantic marriage, wherein some extraordinary focus on the sex act seems to have developed, and the sexual side no longer taken as so ordinary as to need no special attention.

To repeat, even modern people, thoroughly "emancipated" from religion, seem still capable of being awed at their having by their sex act brought a new being into the world.

But it is death which is the greatest of the mysteries and the foremost source of awe among humans. It is also fraught with generous measures of fear.

Why the fear of death? Unquestionably a basis for it is the human observation that often it has a prelude of illness, and sometimes such illness entails unbearable suffering; perhaps it is the fear of undergoing suffering before death that increases the anxiety about death itself. One hears people speak in envy of those who pass away peacefully and suddenly.

But death involves an unknown: What happens to a person after death? Where there is no belief in an afterlife, then the prospect that awaits a person is merely that of oblivion. In some parts of the world, oblivion after death is a welcome prospect; in the western world it defies the capacity of the ordinary man to grasp oblivion as something welcome. This oblivion after death is destined to endure endlessly into the eternal future. (We usually think of time as having somehow begun, and capable of lasting unendingly into the future; it is almost impossible for us to envisage time in the past as having been potentially as endless as time is conceived of respecting the future.)

If it is oblivion that lies in store, then a man's span on earth seems unimportant and even futile. The Book of Ecclesiastes, composed before the Hebrews embraced a belief in an afterlife, makes this point with fullest eloquence; modern translations offer new ways of saying, "Vanity of vanities, all is vanity," such as "Emptiness of emptiness, all is empty," or "Futility of futilities, living is futile," but the meaning is still the same. Ecclesiastes explores the many pursuits of men, the quests for wealth, for power, for royalty, but asserts that he who attains one or all of these ends up in the same cemetery with those who attain nothing.

Curiously, a passage which laments how stale and unprofitable life is, has come to offer comfort to some:

> There is a time to be born, a time to die.
> A time to plant, a time to pluck what was planted...
> A time to love, a time to hate;
> A time for war, a time for peace.
> What gain does the toiler have from his labor?

While this passage (Ecclesiastes 3:2, 8-9) comments bitterly on the essentially humdrum character of living, I have known families who have wanted the passage read at a funeral service, possibly as expressing their form of acquiescing in the inevitable.

Ecclesiastes is not a cheering book; quite the contrary. Its hold on people is possibly the courage of its facing what for the author was the truth, that one can by a pleasant job and by virtuous living be too busy to become preoccupied with the emptiness, the futility of living.

We do not know precisely how the doctrine of an afterlife arose. But here we must pause for the definition of three words. *Eternal life* means that death abstains from coming to a person. (Such might have happened to man, so runs the biblical legend, had he eaten from the tree of life — that is, of eternal life — in the Garden of Eden, Genesis 3:22-24). *Resurrection* is the view that death truly comes, but after some interval life is restored. Resurrection is not the same as a recurrent incident we

87

often hear of, the revival of a person seemingly asphyxiated or drowned, for such a person is not in this sense truly dead. Apparently a person in the ancient Jewish world was deemed truly dead only if he was dead for three days; the traditions about Jesus are that he rose from death *on the third day*. If it had been told as occurring earlier than the third day, the accusation would have been credibly leveled that he was not truly dead.

Immortality is quite different from resurrection. The notion of immortality is that the material side of man (his body, hair, bones) does die, but his soul-spirit does not; rather, at the death of the body, the soul-spirit is released to undergo some destiny other than the burial and decay of the body. A passage in the Reform Jewish Prayerbook reads: "Only the body has died and been laid in the dust. The spirit lives in the shelter of God's love and mercy."*

What *does* happen after death? We do not know. Shakespeare in Hamlet's soliloquy, "To be or not to be," writes:

> Who would these fardels bear,
> To grunt and sweat under a weary life,
> But that the dread of something after death —
> The undiscovered country from whose bourn
> No traveller returns — puzzles the will,
> And makes us rather bear those ills we have
> Than fly to others that we know not of.

(act III, scene I, lines 76-82)

---

*Let the reader be assured, first, that the distinction here given between resurrection and immortality is valid; resurrection is primarily Hebrew, immortality Grecian. Second, medieval scholastics ordinarily "explained" resurrection by making it identical with immortality, with the consequence that the difference tended to become blurred and even disappeared.

As a result, the Religions, in explaining what has happened to the soul in immortality after the death of the body, or what the dead do while awaiting resurrection, have tended to merge resurrection and immortality into one and the same thing.

What have people believed, and why? Some have believed that death is not the end. In certain moods, some have believed that a better world than this vale of tears awaits the dying: "I'm coming, I'm coming to a better world I know." In Jewish lore, the place of the afterlife is a heavenly Garden of Eden.

There are those who have thought that the separation from loved ones caused by death would be followed by a reunion in the afterlife. Ordinarily, people who are hopeful allocate the place of afterlife as "heaven"; fearful people speak of the place as hell, presumably in an underworld (since the dead are buried in the ground).

After a person comes to believe in the afterlife, he ordinarily fashions it in the opposing terms of paradise with its rewards or of hell and its punishments.

Why? There are many reasons that have impelled men to believe in an afterlife. One is that only through such a belief can most men come to terms with the palpable pains, sorrows, injustices and inequities observable in living. A second reason is man's emotional reluctance to agree with Ecclesiastes that life, especially one's own, is futile.* A third reason is the sense of comfort, of assurance that the belief can give, especially to the sick, the old, or the dying.

The terror of dying (as distinct from the understandable terror of dying in pain or in disabling weakness) is irrational. It is especially irrational for a person to believe in God but to hold

*Henry Wadsworth Longfellow, in *A Psalm of Life,* wrote:

> Tell me not, in mournful numbers
>   Life is but an empty dream! —
> For the soul is dead that slumbers,
>   And things are not what they seem.

> Life is real! Life is earnest!
>   And the grave is not the goal;
> Dust thou art, to dust returnest,
>   Was not spoken of the soul.

89

that God is somehow fearful, somehow bent on punishing men, somehow cruel and vindictive. It is true that passages in sacred literature do speak of a terrifying God. On the other hand, the literature speaks even more abundantly of God as a loving father. (Perhaps it is true, as some allege, that we view God as awesome or loving, depending on how each of us viewed his own father.)

I can well understand that complete scoundrels, fearing no man, can come to fear God; I do not fully understand why ordinary people, who are neither saints nor extreme sinners, should fear God. Perhaps some Religions indoctrinate their communicants to fear him and to avoid "sinning," lest sin arouse some fearful divine displeasure. But ordinary people have no reason to fear God. I am not saying that it is abnormal for a person to have passing moments of fear or even critical moments of sheer terror. I am saying that, to the extent that men can think things through, there are viable alternatives to such instinctual fear, in that God might be neither fearful nor loving, or he might be only loving. To fear God is to respond to a bad conscience.

Surely, in view of how many men have already died, one can conclude that all men are somehow capable of undergoing the experience of those who have come before them. Whether death brings only oblivion, or whether, instead, there is an afterlife, one needs to conclude the fear of death, or worse, the terror of dying, seems counter to the accumulated experience and wisdom of the race.

Still another question might be asked: What value to my life is my belief about an afterlife? Does my belief about afterlife constrict me, shrink me, obstruct my self-realization? Or does it motivate me to an increased concern for the welfare of the living? Each person comes to his own conclusion. But surely what we believe about death affects how we live — much more than does any other belief.

Birth, marriage, and death are the milestones that impinge on us more than all the other events. It is these which can tend to shape what we believe; in turn, what we believe shapes what we do with our lives.

XIV

Mysticism

AS WE HUMANS vary in our dispositions towards money, politics, literature, and so on, so also do we vary in our dispositions to religion. Let us envisage two people, both of them by their own proclamation religious and both faithful communicants. Both conform, willingly and gladly, to the external requirements of their denomination. One, observing the rites and ceremonies, finds his personal needs completely met by such observance, and is never aware of any personal sense of having been, as it were, touched by God. The other, however, feels that he has recurrently been so touched. The first is deeply moved by the rituals, but by disposition does not proceed beyond them; the second, moved by the rituals, has an inner feeling which, in intensity, goes beyond his being touched by the rituals. To say this in another way, one person reads the prayerbook happily and dutifully but is essentially only reading, while the other, in his reading the prayerbook, is praying — that is, speaking to God. Some Religions offer a broad, vast range of ritual (e.g., traditional Judaism or Roman Catholicism), but others offer a minimum, as is characteristic of Protestants, especially Quakers, who have virtually no rituals, but hold a "first day" meeting with the hope and expectation that the worshipers will come to feel some "inner light." There are, of course, many gradations between these extremes, and, indeed, there are those who feel, in all honesty, that ritual is an obstruction to the sense of being touched by God, rather than a means of furthering this sense. Religious rituals arose historically as a means of bringing the deity and the worshiper into close connection, but there is a universal tendency for rituals to become ends in themselves. The Hebrew prophets in pre-exilic times eloquently rejected ritual as a distortion of true religion, and some modern people do the same, but ritual need not distort.

The difference between the person satisfied by ritual or external observance and the one who feels a sense of being touched by God is largely a matter of degree and of personal make-up. (While this difference is noticeable, one can often make too much of it.) We call the person who feels touched by God a *mystic*. Naturally, there are different forms of mysticism, and there are many varieties that have appeared at different times and places.

But we must here pause to consider the word *intuition*. It implies reaching a conclusion without going through the usual logical steps involved to get there. It is encountered in such experiences as the brilliant math student or chess player who assesses a problem with such lightning speed that the rest of us explain his achievement as "intuition." A teacher sees this very often in some of his best students.

Intuition is in one sense like a guess but is in reality more like an "educated guess" than the mere fumbling that the word *guess* can imply. Intuition, like the guess, can be wrong, for to avoid a step-wise procedure can be hazardous. A reliance on intuition is precarious. But intuition is also at times right. In games of bridge or chess, some intuitive players remember, analyze, and reach a right conclusion with greatest celerity, but others simply play wildly.

Intuition in the sense of a rapid, correct grasp of data and of their meaning is a capacity characteristic of some people. Accordingly, in the view of the Greeks, the process of achieving personal perfection involved the ability to learn, the ability to put learning to practice, and, as a third, intuition; the latter would not have been included unless it had seemed to be a widespread human characteristic. Perhaps enough has been said to establish intuition as a recurrent human characteristic.

93

In the religious usage, intuition is a direct grasp of the meaning of God, and mysticism is an intuitive sense of communion with him, independent of any ritual, and equally independent of steps of logic.

The word *mysticism* is used about the Hebrew prophets in the sense of their direct and intuitive entry into a vivid relationship with God. The uniqueness in prophetic mysticism is that it was not portrayed as silent; rather, the biblical books report that the deity spoke to the prophet, and some prophets to the deity, in a two-way conversation — this in clear, communicable words. Perhaps we might differentiate between silent mysticism and the prophetic.*

We do not today fully understand the nature of the biblical prophetic experience, despite efforts, especially by some psychologists, to explain it. The question is put in this way: Did a man such as Amos or Isaiah believe that he was hearing clear words from the deity, as each of them reports? Or, is it reasonable to suppose that an inner sense or feeling, or intuition, led an Amos or Isaiah to translate into clear words what was only some subjective sense or feeling? There are those who incline to such an explanation, and it may be right, but it is clearly far removed from the form of the experience narrated in Scripture. The Religions, however, have felt the need to contend that prophecy was possible (and, so it is maintained, credible) in the past, but that it has ceased as a phenomenon, usually because later generations through sinfulness have forfeited the privilege.

It is a reality that the ancient Hebrew literary prophets were men of surpassing poetic gifts and of tremendous insight, so that interpreters of Scripture incline to separate them from the "whirling dervishes" occasionally there described and from the court sycophants who could tell a monarch what the outcome of some crisis or military engagement would be. Some interpreters

---

*Some scholars needlessly dispute whether to classify biblical prophets as mystics or not; to such scholars the prophets merely represent a manifestation of mysticism so unique as to merit a classification of its own.

wish to shield an Amos or Isaiah, with their perceptive denunciations of social injustice, from being identified with fortune-tellers, and allude (correctly) to the freedom of the great prophets (Amos, Hosea, Isaiah, Micah, Jeremiah) from the magic rigamarole of the dervish; an old cliché describes these men as "forth-tellers," rather than "fore-tellers." Yet, even one who admires the biblical prophets without reservation ought not, in all honesty, deny that they were partially "fore-tellers"; it was not the crass, commercial "foretelling" of the dervish, but, nevertheless, it was foretelling.

Whether or not God truly spoke to the great prophets is a matter of belief. To repeat, we do not fully or accurately understand the phenomenon. Perhaps the closest we can come is an important observation: mysticism, whether prophetic or silent, is always conditioned by the environment, and in an age when foretelling was readily accepted by the populace, the phenomenon of prophecy was neither strange nor out of keeping with the times.

There are some personalities of prominence who are silent mystics — Thomas à Kempis, Francis of Assisi, the Baal Shem Tov (the founder of Hassidism), and George Fox. Scholars have classified these people and arranged the attributes common to these and other mystics into various logical categories. What one might say is the common characteristic for all these eminent, admirable mystics has been the way, differing only in degree, in which each has felt that he was losing himself in God. Such mystics have ordinarily asserted that the experience of God is beyond their expressing in words.

There have, however, been mystics who later turn to a literary expression which does not attempt to describe the experience itself, but that which has ensued as a direct consequence of it.

In a general way, it can be said that mystics turn inward to confront the mysteries of living and discover, in their solitude or achieved isolation, a means of either escaping from or of coping with the external world. An ancient writer used as a description of the mystic experience the striking phrase, "sober intoxication."

A Latin phrase, *unio mystica*, has been widely used as describing the joining of the soul-spirit of man with God. The Christian ritual of "communion" — also called the "Eucharist" and the "Lord's supper" — in which bread (or a wafer) is eaten, and wine is drunk, was considered to be more than a memorial of Jesus, indeed, a way of mystical union with him, for the bread was symbolic of his body and the wine of his blood; the worshiper who partook thereby entered into the union. In the sixteenth century, the Catholic Church emphasized that miraculously the wafer and the wine were changed into the real body and blood of the Christ. Some Protestant churches hold a comparable belief in the miraculous transformation of the wafer and the wine; other Protestant churches regard the ritual as only a vivid memorial of Jesus.

The mystic moment, so it appears, can come to a person while praying or going through a ritual in a sanctuary, or while walking in the woods or standing on a seashore. It seems to be able either to burst forcefully upon a person or else gently to infuse him. It seems at times to last no longer than the proverbial split-second, or else it may endure for a matter of moments. It is frequently associated with silent prayer.

The point is that a person does not live unbrokenly in a mystical state unless he is pathological. That is why we speak of being "touched" by God. What can last long is not the mystic moment itself but the effect of it. The experience seems capable of raising one's dedication to social values, strengthening one's moral fiber, or altering a person from wavering into resolute determination.

It can also seduce a person into arrogance, fashion him into a bigot, and debase him into a fanatic.

What it seems to do is to heighten personality traits that antecedently may have been only latent or recessive.

The mystic moment is potentially a noble experience, but all too often it has been utilized ignobly.

Since it is natural for men to try to explain all phenomena, especially those of religion, the Religions have included philosophers who have wished to explain exactly how the soul-spirit can become free from the bodily prison in order to undergo union with God. Such philosophers have tried to provide a rational analysis of the intuitive personal feeling in order to understand it as possibly universal among men. More than one philosopher, himself devoid of mystical experience, has tried to "explain" mysticism. One wonders if such philosophers succeed!

At times there have been those who have wanted to utilize either music or the burning of incense as a means of inducing mystic experience. In the past ten years, LSD has been used; indeed some scholars have wondered whether medieval mystics used drugs to induce their experience. But ordinarily by mysticism we mean something entirely inner, not connected directly with any specific ritual or device of any kind.

Most of us ordinary people, however deeply touched by God we may at some moment be, scarcely qualify as full-fledged mystics. Some people have, at most, recurrent "experiences" that may in one way or other affect their lives, but not to the point of taking them out of our ordinary routines and customary employment.

The reality of the matter seems to be this: in our age we are so antimiracle and so naturalistic that we are suspicious of the person we consider a mystic; hence we do not wish to expose to public knowledge (and public ridicule) whatever quasi-mystical experiences we ourselves may have. We preserve such experiences as part of what is the most private of all our privacies, as if to declare them openly is tantamount to debasing and terminating them. All this is readily to be understood, for none of us wants to be regarded as peculiar, or a lunatic, or a religious fanatic.

Then, very well, let privacy be maintained.

But that person whose disposition is such that the mystic moment is a real experience for him is ill-advised to blunt or suppress it, for such a religious experience would appear consistent with his personality. Only, let such a person not suppose — as so many quasimystics seem to do — that one is thereby loftier and more authentically religious than the nonmystic. The best of the authentic mystics possessed a laudable measure of humility.

XV

Creeds and Dogmas

ONE OF THE MOST admirable aspects of human life is the infinite variety of people and personalities. Some people like music, some fishing, some to play chess, and some to garden. One of the least admirable aspects of human life is a tendency on the part of some to suppose that their particular response is the only one, or the only right one, and all others are wrong. So, too, in religion. So, too, even in the Religions.

Let us imagine that some new religion has come into being. It has moved from a founder, through his followers, their followers, and theirs, and has become somewhat sizable and stable. Inevitably, differing responses to the content of the new religion will arise; there will be people who hold that theirs is the only proper response and all others are improper. A system of officials may wish to decide which of the various responses is the right one; strife among factions may prompt these officials to make an urgent decision. In any corporate entity — whether a religion, a political party, or a social club — comparable situations arise. Ordinarily a tacit issue lies in the background: Is there room for diversity, and, if so, how much?

Again, as the religion has grown in size, and reached the stage where people have been born into it and children reared within it, a natural tendency is for some relatively short statement of the principles of the religion to be formed, or at least for some of the key ideas to become expressed in a series of striking phrases. Such a brief statement is called a *creed*.

Dogma basically means "a teaching." In a religion, when a

99

diversity of views arise, they can readily clash with each other. If a mechanism is available (such as a meeting of designated officials) a decision is possible whether the diversity is tolerable or not. If it does not seem tolerable, then usually something seems necessary to do.

Creed and dogma are normal in virtually all religions. The particular *form* in which a creed or a dogma can emerge differs in religions; creed and dogma in Christendom are different from those in Judaism.

Judaism has had its distinctive beliefs. It has not had an explicit creed; it has utilized the biblical phrase, "Hear, O Israel, the Lord our God, the Lord is one," as the equivalent. The Hebrew for "hear" is *shma*, by which the whole sentence is known. The *shma* became equivalent to a creed when Judaism, moving into the Greco-Roman world, encountered religions which were not monotheistic, and also when types of thinking about God that seemed inconsistent with monotheism entered into Judaism. The *shma* was used to assert the Jewish conception of monotheism in response to polytheism from outside or to a "tinkering" with monotheism from within. In time, the *shma* became the brief way of a Jew's expressing the full array of his Jewish loyalties, so that a child was taught it as his nightly prayer and a dying person repeated it as a profession of his faith in God. Judaism, however, did not develop a longer creed as did Christianity, nor did it approach dogmas in the same way as did Christians. (We will return to the Jewish way.)

Central to Christianity is the double view that Jesus died and was resurrected and that there was profound significance for mankind in his death and resurrection. From both Jews and pagans, there came denials of the credibility of these claims about Jesus; from within Christendom a troubling diversity of views arose about him. These diverse views focused on the question of whether Jesus had been truly *human*.* Was Jesus a hu-

---

*In the past two hundred years, diverse views have existed on the question, Was Jesus truly divine? Early disputes — bitter ones — were on whether he

man being like other human beings, differing from them in that he was also divine, or was he less than fully human? There were those who denied that he had been fully human; some even carried their denial to the point of holding that he had been an *apparition*, not a physical, tangible man. Was such diversity tolerable in Christendom?

One more factor about Christianity must be noted. Christianity was originally a Jewish movement, a legatee of the Jewish view that God had revealed through Moses the laws by which men should live. The apostle Paul (I repeat here) rejected the view that laws, even those of Moses, could be the ultimate, the highest form of religion; in his view, the ultimate form was a man's total and unreserved reliance on God. Paul "proved" his case by citing that in the Bible, Abraham, living long before Moses, was able to attain righteousness, having done so through his *faith* in God. Hence, faith — complete reliance on God — was attested to in Scripture as a means of achieving righteousness. The later laws coming from Moses were a descent from the high point earlier attained by Abraham; with the advent of Jesus, men were wondrously able to attain righteousness as Abraham had — by faith — and not by obedience to laws. According to Paul, the interval when the laws were useful or valid had now ended. In a word, Paul proposed faith as a higher means of conforming to God's will than was conforming to the Mosaic laws. Let us emphasize that the word *faith* in Paul's use meant complete reliance on God.

But later Christians altered the sense of the word *faith*, taking it to mean "that which is credible, that which Christians should believe." For example, Should Christians believe that Jesus was not truly human? Was such a belief admissible, was it proper? Out of such questioning, a second step took place in Christianity: the emergence of the view that some beliefs were admissible, and some definitely not. That is, a distinction arose between

---

was truly human, for the ancient disputants within the church all accepted his divinity.

"proper" and "improper" faith. In Judaism the key question was, What is the proper way of observing the laws? The key question in Christianity was, What is the proper set of beliefs, the proper faith? Judaism seems to have been content with a bare assertion of monotheism; Christians were under the urgent need to define faith in detail.

Until Christianity developed its own inner organization, with designated officials, it could not come to authoritative decisions on matters of proper faith. For a quite extended period, from about A.D. 40 to 325, individual Christians could propose what seemed the proper faith, and they could attack and denounce formulations from others that to them seemed improper. Two words arose in the often heated exchanges: orthodoxy ("the proper teaching") and heresy ("the improper view of a willful group"). In A.D. 325, the Roman emperor Constantine assembled Christian bishops to a "council" at Nicea in Asia Minor. Among other business transacted, there was a decision reached about the views of a certain Arius who held that Jesus was of a substance similar to God but not identical with God. At Nicea, Arius was voted to be a heretic, and his views a heresy. Moreover, the power of the emperor was available to compel Christians to believe in accordance with the decision which was passed and to punish and exterminate those who held Arian views. What is to be noticed here is that an officialdom was by now at hand to be summoned, so that a divisive matter could be debated and voted on, and thereafter the power of government was available to try to enforce the decision.

In Christendom, a creed is an authoritative, brief statement of the proper belief. Several such creeds have come down to us from the fourth and fifth centuries: the earliest is the Nicene (sometimes spelled Nicean); next came the Apostles' Creed; and then the Athanasian. They were designed to be easily learned and absorbed; children could be taught them, and adults could use them as the equivalent of a prayer. The classic creeds grew out of hymn-like passages in the New Testament about the Christ. Here is a version of the Nicene Creed:

102

We believe

I. In one God the Father Almighty, maker of heaven and earth, and of all things visible and invisible.

II. And in one Lord Jesus Christ, the only begotten Son of God, begotten of His Father before all worlds, God of God, light of light, very God of very God; begotten, not made; being of one substance with the Father; by whom all things were made;

Who for us men and for our salvation came down from heaven, and was incarnate by the Holy Ghost of the Virgin Mary, and was made man:

And was crucified also for us under Pontius Pilate;*

He suffered and was buried, and

The third day He rose again, according to the Scriptures:

And ascended into heaven, and sitteth on the right hand of the Father,

And He shall come again, with glory, to judge both the quick and the dead, whose kingdom shall have no end.

III. And in the Holy Ghost, the Lord and Giver of Life, who proceedeth from the Father and the Son, who with the Father and the Son together is worshipped and glorified; who spoke by the prophets:

One Catholic and Apostolic Church;

We acknowledge one baptism for remission of sins:

We look for the resurrection of the dead:

And the life of the world to come.

A dogma is an ad hoc decision by an authoritative Christian body, such as a convened council. It is a teaching the acceptance of which is obligatory on the faithful, such as the Immaculate Conception (1854), or the infallability of the Pope (1870). The totality of the authoritative, obligatory teaching of the church is "the dogma."†

Creed and dogma, in the sense of explicit, defined, and ob-

---

*This passage is regarded as opposing the view that Jesus was only an apparition or only a symbolic man. The allusion to Pontius Pilate implies that Jesus lived in a particular time and place, something denied by those who viewed him as an apparition or only a symbolic man.

†We speak of a person as dogmatic, in a quite unflattering sense, when we see in him a compulsion to have his opinion prevail over the opinions of others, not because he is right, but because he simply needs to prevail.

Catholic scholars (quite averse to such unbecoming "dogmatism") defend

ligatory beliefs, are characteristically Christian. Hence, since secular authority became available to Christendom in the fourth century, it possessed the power to compel acceptance and to punish those Christians who directly or indirectly held dissenting beliefs. Creed and dogma have characterized numerous Protestant communions, many of which have devised their own formulations, such as the thirty-nine Articles of the Church of England and the twenty-four Articles of Religion of the Methodists.

Classic instances of the treatment of heretics have been the cruelties of the Inquisition,* the burning to death of the Czech John Hus in 1415, the Italian Giordano Bruno in 1600, and the Protestant Michael Servetus by other Protestants in Geneva in 1553. The burning of heretics was legal in England until 1704.

Since secular power is no longer available to church authorities, excommunication, that is, expulsion and exclusion from a church, has become the maximum recourse available.

Judaism never developed universal authorities comparable to the Pope and the College of Cardinals; it has never had a worldwide ("ecumenical") gathering such as the Councils which Catholics convened at Nicea, at Trent in the sixteenth century, or at Rome in 1870 and in the 1960s. It has lacked counterparts to the Christian creeds† and dogmas. It has lacked, except in some local areas, persons with authority *over* the tradi-

---

dogma on the basis that dogmas explain and define those ideas which embody the revealed truths of the Church. For such scholars, dogma is more essentially an explanation than an obligatory teaching.

*A heretic was burned at the stake after a public procession to the stake, a sermon, and the lighting of the fire; this was termed an *auto da fe*, "an act of faith."

†The eminent Spanish rabbi, Maimonides (1135-1204), composed a list of thirteen articles which for him seemed to summarize Judaism, and couched it in credal form. It was not, however, proposed to or accepted at a convened council; it was opposed by some eminent sages, but became widely accepted by many Jews and was incorporated into some versions of the Jewish prayerbook. Hence, the Creed of Maimonides is both like and yet unlike Christian creeds.

tion, for a rabbi had authority only *in* the tradition and never equality with it or superiority over it. This is the case because, for the most part, Judaism left the details of faith to remain undefined. On the other hand, definitions and prescriptions about laws and derivative laws became minutely defined. The Christian term *orthodoxy* has been applied to traditional Judaism, but, as many have noted, the word is really misapplied; a better term might be "orthoproxy," which would mean that Judaism has demanded proper practice of, and obedience to, the Mosaic law and its defining derivatives. (Dogmatism has been quite as readily available in the Jewish scheme of things as in the Christian.)

What troubles modern men about creeds and dogma? Perhaps foremost is that obligatory belief goes against the grain of man's dedication to the freedom for one to think as one sees fit.

Next, if one would assume that one is (or ought to be) free to choose whether to believe or not, surely a prerequisite is that one understand what one is or is not choosing. The creeds and the dogmas simply do not say fully intelligible things to modern man. The creeds were shaped over fifteen hundred years ago, in the Near East, in a setting in which prevailed a world view which could scarcely have been more different from ours. I have put a footnote on one passage in the creed reproduced above; let me ask: What modern person would, or could, say in honesty that he thoroughly understands that creed in toto? Could he, or would he, say in honesty that though he does not understand some of the details, he nevertheless grasps the general tenor and import? Somewhere between tragic and comic have been some efforts in the Religions to explain their creeds, and I must run the risk of seeming to be arrogant in saying that most of the explanations I have seen have not been explanations at all but simply justifications. How adept the explainers have been at speaking to the already persuaded, and how they fall short of any ability (and probably any desire) to speak to the unpersuaded — even to those eager to be persuaded!

105

The case is scarcely different with dogmas — whether Catholic or Protestant abstractions or the obstruseness and "legal-fictions" of Judaism. Modern men scarcely progress to the point of choosing to accept or reject them, for they remain adrift in noncomprehension. Yet even understanding creed and dogma need not lead to acquiescence, for the vital concerns of a modern man can feel very remote from the urgent crisis centuries ago when a particular Christian dogma or Jewish law emerged, and modern man can feel no sense of sharing in the achievement of decision which in its time a dogma or a new law represented. Modern men, even with the best good will, can feel that the content of a dogma is outmoded and of no palpable concern to him.

Lastly, the splits in Judaism, and those in Christendom between Catholicism and Protestantism, and the fragmentation of Protestantism have created an impression of utter chaos. In Christendom, Protestants have rejected Catholic dogmas but settled on their own, these in endless shapes and forms; Catholics have responded to the Protestant reformation and to the post-enlightenment world of the nineteenth and twentieth centuries with fresh dogmas.

Moreover, there is in the Religions some fear that novelty is destructive of the truth of the inherited faith. Seldom do responsible religious authorities seem ready to admit openly and honestly that they are ever altering anything from the past; rather, the procedure in the Religions is to disguise an innovation or an alteration by agile words which seek to show that the innovation, "properly understood," is a legacy from the ancient past, now newly examined; hence, an adopted alteration is no alteration at all, only a "clarification" of a matter hoary with age. Again, a favorite device of the Religions is to pick on some term, divest it of its natural and historic meaning, then read a new meaning into it, and thereafter proceed to use the term with such ambiguity that it seems to carry both the ancient and the revised meaning, however contradictory these may be.

Simplicity and directness are notably absent — and modern men, by and large, feel no bond for or sense of continuity with the creeds and dogmas, even when, sitting in the pew of a church or synagogue, they may join in some recitation.

I am not prepared to sanction or defend any compulsions, direct or indirect, in matters of religion. I abhor the persecutions and killings in the name of religion, and have no impulse to defend them. I have written elsewhere that religion has represented both the very best and the very, very worst in the course of European history.

Yet let me say a few words in defense of aspects of the impulse towards creed and dogma. Men are entitled to explanations, and a Religion owes it to its communicants to explain to them what the Religion has meant and what it means. Insofar as creeds do this, and dogmas clarify uncertainties, they are urgent necessities to Religions. But these need to exist in terms of strictest honesty, without compulsions of any kind.*

Moreover, let the Religions admit honestly that they have changed, are changing, and will change. Let the spokesman admit to the reality of change without shilly-shally. And let them be honest enough in their self-searching to admit the recurrent necessity of change. Surely even the most unbending of traditionalists can understand that it is only the dead religions that are free of change.

Let creed and dogma be the voluntary offerings of the Religions, to the end of enlightening its communicants.

And let excommunication perish quickly. Obviously I do not mean that any assembled body ought not have the right to protect its quiet from a pathological nuisance who wanders in. I

---

*I have heard it said that few things are as senseless as a person's intoning in a pew words he neither believes in nor understands. In a sense, this is right. But such a view can be hasty and superficial, for it can overlook the emotional need that such participation in public worship affords. There is all the difference in the world between a person's private recitation of what he does not believe in or understand and his doing so in a public worship, as I set forth on page 119.

107

have in mind, rather, the dispositions that have existed to put people into intellectual straightjackets in the name of fidelity to the legacy a Religion has had from the past. The Religions can readily afford the heretics and the heresies; the Religions have paid a higher price for expelling them than they would have paid in tolerating them.

If a person feels that his convictions compel him to leave a Religion, and he has inquired adequately, then let him leave. But let the Religions not push him out or speed him on his way.

Edward Markham, in "Outwitted," wrote:

> He drew a circle that shut me out —
> Heretic, rebel, a thing to flout.
> But Love and I had the wit to win;
> We drew a circle that took him in.

XVI

Piety

NO WORDS that I know are as treacherous as *pious* and *piety*. The root meaning suggests devout reverence towards God, surely an admirable quality. The words, however, have acquired quite a negative overtone, as though piety is inevitably a matter of external show, composed of generous measures of stupidity, intolerance, and hypocrisy. In my experience the words are used favorably about elderly persons whom one knows only to a limited extent, for piety has come to be something we are prepared to forgive if only we are not unduly exposed to the pious.

Moreover, the tests of piety in the past have seemed to suppose that enjoyment, humor, and laughter are innately antireligious. Piety has seemed to mean a need to deny one's self ordinary sensual pleasures, and to eat stale crumbs and drink tepid water — in short, to mortify the body. Piety has seemed to mean unending solemnity, ponderous thinking, and even more ponderous speaking (hence the "pulpit voice"), and a general supposition that God is somehow better served if only one does not enjoy oneself in doing so. The short step between sanctity and sanctimoniousness comes all too easily to some people, and there are those incapable of assessing holiness except as being "holier than thou." How readily those who try for righteousness become selfrighteous!

The modern age has only a grudging respect (mingled with contempt) for piety. That this is so broadly the case is, moreover, a commentary on the role played by the Religions on too many historic occasions. Wars and persecutions and obstructions to intellectual freedom and the suppression of individual rights are so easily documented in the history of the Religions that for the ordinary person the affirmative contributions of the Religions tend to be forgotten or else regarded as insignificant compared with the harm they have done. The pious person appears to be not the devout believer in God but, instead, the person ready to enlist in the baleful deeds of the Religions.

Less frighteningly, a pious person can seem to us to have an idiosyncracy we are willing for him to possess — but only if we are free from it or from excessive contact with him. The pious person seems obsessed with the minutiae required or advocated by his Religion, and his preoccupations can strike us as little better than trivial. Even when, in our condescension, we trust the earnestness of a pious man, we are still prepared to convict him of a certain eccentricity, and we usually refrain from attributing genuine profundity to his earnestness; the word *misguided* trips to our tongue. Moreover, we can find ourselves chagrined and embarrassed if we have frequent dealings with him.

I do not write to commend our scorn of the pious, but only to report its widespread character. I have heard such scorn in many places — Norway, Denmark, Germany, Britain, Israel, and the United States.

It is only scorn, and not hatred, that marks our attitude. Moreover, it is a scorn directed at a lay person who is a communicant of a Religion, not one of its clergymen. For the latter there is a comparable feeling of contempt that goes by the half-forgotten name of anticlericalism. One might best describe anticlericalism as the feeling that the Religions are all right, but the clergy are not. Historically, the clergy were granted special legal privileges and immunities (called "benefits of clergy"); they, not ordinary communicants, led the Religions into their historic misdeeds. They fostered the persecutions, they justified the intolerances; they led governments to burn people at the stake for

110

heresy or to kill old women on the charge of being witches. They were the ones who stood in the way of progress, who supported tyrants in their claim to the "divine rights" of kings, and who used their offices to influence governments or to demand special rights for their church, or to obstruct education, or to sabotage or destroy labor unions. The ordinary middle class man a century ago came to conceive of the clergy as the foe of all that was good, progressive, democratic, and tolerant.

Anticlericalism has especially flourished in European countries where there has been a state religion, and in those countries, like France, where a single Religion has claimed the overwhelming majority of the inhabitants. In many European countries, the anticlericalism which was at its height in the nineteenth century has receded into a mere indifference on the part of people to the clergy. Active, vivid anticlericalism is in our day most discernible in Israel; there a complicated political alignment between the Ben Gurion-Golda Meir Socialist party and the Orthodox Religious party has resulted in a government which is moderately socialist but able to stay in power only by abdicating to the Religious Party a control over the country's religious affairs. The Ministry of Religion and its accompanying rabbinate are the bête-nôire of most Israelis. (On my first visit to Jerusalem, arriving in a *sherut* cab, the driver spat contemptuously when he drove past the Ministry, and then eloquently expounded on his contempt of it.)

In my experience, no country that I know of is as free of anticlericalism as the United States. In our country, the attendance at public worship exceeds in percentage the attendance in European countries, especially the Protestant ones. But Americans seem broadly to believe that a clergyman has a specific role, limited to administering religious rites, and that "he has no business getting into politics"; the latter cry increases when a clergyman, or association of them, takes a public stand on divisive issues, whether integration, the Viet Nam war, or the right to buy alcoholic beverages.

111

There has been a broad feeling among us that piety and the pious are a barrier to normal human enjoyment. It is not too long ago — I can personally remember this — when Sunday movies and baseball were illegal. It was the pious who have taken the lead in barring what ordinary people regard as harmless pleasures; piety has come to be identified with senseless self-denials.*

Shall we suppress our own tendencies to devoutness because there are and have been devout people we cannot admire? Must piety inevitably be a trivialization of religion? Is piety "true piety" because it is humorless, lugubrious, ostentatious? Surely we can be patriots even when we witness patrioteering and abstain from it, and surely we can be decent citizens even though there are indecent Watergates in Washington, in state capitols, and county seats.

The misdeeds, hypocrisies, and flagrant irreligion of religious people ought to warn us against our own possible abuse of religion. But the abuses are not a persuasive argument against piety; they are an argument against superficial or false or empty piety.

To avoid the word pious may be natural to us. To avoid piety — true devoutness — is to deny ourselves a realizable human achievement. It is to impoverish ourselves.

True piety implies a rounded person, grateful for his body as well as for his mind, a person able to be light and frivolous when lightness and frivolity are in order, and serious or even solemn, when these are called for. True piety is the active enjoyment of one's life, in a context of worthy purposes and sturdy convic-

---

*Protestants and Jews, while respecting the celibacy of Catholic priests and nuns, seldom understand it sympathetically; and the somewhat abundant defection of priests and nuns into marriage in recent times confirms non-Catholics in their thoughtless disdain of celibacy.

112

tions about what is right and wrong, and a sense of attunement to the mysteries of living.*

*A few words here about profanity as impiety: Our age has inherited a tradition that the open pronunciation of certain holy words is an affront to God, that an act of profanation ("making common") of the holy is involved. Some medieval words, such as *zounds* and *bloody* were deemed sinful to use, zounds being shortened from "Jesus' wounds" and bloody from an oath "by the lady," that is, by Mary. It is Christianity in particular where the tradition of abstaining from profanity has flourished. It derives in part from Matthew 12:31, "Whoever speaks against the Holy Spirit will not be forgiven, either in this age or in the age to come." The "sin against the holy ghost" has been interpreted by Christians as meaning the use of profanity. In the Victorian age, the disapproval of profanity was extended to the four-letter words for the human anatomy and physiology. I have no patience with the supposition that mere words can work magic and no tolerance for an intolerance of these words.

But I have even less patience with the needless use of profanity or fourletter words as in modern literature, plays, and movies. Their needless use betrays a laziness or lack of inventiveness on the part of the author. The overuse of them is kindred to the overuse of colorful adjectives and adverbs in precious writing, wherein a surfeit of unnecessary modifiers dilutes and destroys the literary effect. Had we not our heritage of abstaining in polite society from these words (and that was wrong), we would not need to veer to the other swing of the pendulum and use them overabundantly. I do not think that hearing these words shocks or startles me; rather, I feel impelled to consider humdrum a person who speaks only with these words. They are, in my view, not an affront to God, but to what seems to me an attainable fluency or even commendable elegance.

113

XVII

Personal and Communal Religion

HUMAN INSTITUTIONS are remarkably gifted at getting in the way of their avowed purpose or purposes. Sometimes this is a result of growth in size and the operation of Parkinson's law; sometimes an institution becomes diverted from its proper function (as universities, through football, have intruded into public entertainment); sometimes highly placed individuals distort an institution into a means of personal aggrandizement. The Religions have not escaped these pitfalls, especially the misdeeds of the officialdom. Wicked as secular politicians are, true wickedness is at its height when a church politician is on the scene, and few denominational officials escape the stigma of being politicians.

The inevitable questions arise: Is an institution truly necessary for those purposes which it avows? For example: Can a person become educated — educated is different from being schooled! — without going to school? Again: Is it possible to distinguish, in the preoccupations of an institution, between what is essential and what is peripheral or dispensable?

Do universities require, as American ones seem to feel, a gymnasium and obligatory classes in physical education? European universities have gotten along without these. Does an art museum require an elaborate structure, or is something more modest sufficient, with more money spent on contents and their exhibition, than on huge facades and enormous lobbies?

There has been no dearth of critics who have deplored the waste by governments or have been startled by recurrent exposures

114

of dishonesty. Universities have been seriously challenged, not only by students in their uprisings but by educators from within the universities. Our public school systems are under severe attack. But I know of no one who thinks seriously that governments or universities ought to disappear. Ordinarily the necessity of governments and universities is conceded even by the severest critics.

It seems to be institutional, organized religion alone which so many modern men view as dispensable. In part, there are those who contend in all earnestness that historically the Religions have done more harm than good. In part, there are those who seek to distinguish between what is presumed essential and what is peripheral or dispensable; they contend that the essential element in religion is the personal, private relationship between a person and God, and that the institutions are not needed. The latter conclusion seems to become reinforced when a person attends public worship and discovers himself exposed to such infelicities as a cacophonic choir, an inept organist, a sermon of low intellectual quality, and the sheer routinization of the worship. In our time, our young people have fashioned new modes of worship in what they ordinarily call *creative services*; a better term might be *experimental*. A guitar, or several, seems more desirable than an organ, and blue jeans seem to be better "Sunday-go-to-meetin' clothes" than the traditional ways of getting dressed up.

Now, the criticism of the Religions is usually justified. It is, though, a mark of the peculiarities of our age that we are more forgiving of the admitted inadequacies of government and universities than of the Religions. We demand of the latter a perfection that we do not demand elsewhere. And we seldom ask what it is one should reasonably expect from a church or a synagogue. I hear people, otherwise generous, complain about the ugliness of having a collection plate or the impersonality of the arrangement of an annual dues for synagogue membership.*

*Christians and Jews use the word *member* in quite different senses. When a

115

I have known people who for a wedding or a funeral in their family want the church or synagogue facilities to be available for their use, as if these can exist without financial support to pay for light, heat, and janitorial services. Such people want to get for free what other people have been willing to pay for.

It is my opinion that a person can be fully religious without ever entering a church or synagogue.* It is my opinion, too, that personal religion is worthier than institutional. But I see absolutely no basis for regarding the institutional and the personal as necessary contradictions, and no reason at all for supposing that one must choose between them. In short, sympathizing with those who authentically cultivate their personal religion, I believe too that they are not fair to or perceptive regarding the institutional forms.

Such people have in my hearing cited the passage in Micah 6:6-8; it runs:

> With what shall I come before the Lord,
>   and bow before God on high?
> Shall I come before him with burnt offerings,
>   with calves a year old?
> Will the Lord be pleased with thousands of rams,
>   with ten thousand rivers of oil? . . .
> He has showed you, O man, what is good
>   and what the Lord requires of you:
> Only to do justice, and love kindness,
>   and walk humbly with your God.

Jew is a member of a synagogue, it means only that he is enrolled as a dues-payer; a Protestant can mean by *member* that he has had a personal inner experience that has changed him from a nominal adherent of Christian beliefs into a personally transformed one. Similarly, Jews use *convert* as meaning a withdrawal from one Religion and entrance into another; many Christians mean by the term that personal experience which changes a person from nominal adherence into a transformed one.

*I would modify this only respecting an affiliation with that kind of church which stipulates attendance at its worship as a requirement; a person unwilling to meet this requirement is scarcely justified in continuing his affiliation.

I personally have no interest in animal sacrifice, a function which the ancient Hebrew priests performed. But it was priests (as a British scholar noted correctly) who preserved the words of Micah and other prophets, and had there been no priests, those words might well have perished. Institutional religion may perpetuate much that is faulty, but it is also a significant — and at times the sole — means of preserving what is valuable.

That the religious institution tends to foster a discouraging routine is true. The Religions which have a prayerbook (Judaism and the Episcopal Church, for example) are bound to strike some modern people as fostering a mechanical sort of thing, in which prayers are read (read, not prayed!) in parrot-like fashion. This is true. But one must be fair: In the Religions there is no dearth of exhortation against the merely mechanical. Jews, for example, inherit the term *kavanah* ("intention"), which is a commended attitude exactly the opposite of mere mechanical reading. From within the Religion there have been voices that have spoken out against fixed prayer, against fixed prayer periods (such as Sabbath morning worship), and even against supposing that some one day (a Sabbath or a festival) is better than some other day.* The Religions have themselves preserved such acute and sensible observations. Yet they have gravitated towards fixity, and have created or reshaped some annual set of recurring holy days. Why? Simply because men in general have a bent for such fixity. It is the rare person who can pursue and cultivate a personal religion with profundity. More say they do than actually do.

It is a reality that our good intentions are not matched by our performances — we forget, we delay, we defer, we neglect. The institutions act on our behalf to remind us and to spur us on.

Moreover, there is a sense in which, under favorable conditions, a public worship provides something that personal religion usually lacks. Plays and movies we have seen, which caused us to

*The Quakers do not use, in their religious life, the words Sunday, Monday, and the like. They call Sunday, "First Day"; Monday, "Second Day"; and so on.

117

rock with laughter or have moved us to tears, do not affect us so intensely if the theater is mostly empty; the movie farces that beguile us in a crowded theater become only silly when we see them on our bedroom television set. There is an added something in the concert hall quite beyond what we experience even from the best and most expensive high fidelity system. That extra something comes from undergoing an emotional experience together with other people.

So, too, does public worship, under favorable circumstances, have a plus that private devotions can lack. In Judaism, the synagogue is a supplement to the home, and private prayer as worthy as public. But certain occasions, for example, the observance of the anniversary of the death of a member of the family (*yahrzeit*), are prescribed for the communal worship. The reason for this is not to my knowledge given, but presumably it rests on the sound observation that grief, if shared, becomes more tolerable.

If we are stingy, we can justify our stinginess by scorning the Religions as unworthy of our financial support. If we are lazy, we can justify our laziness by finding God at home as readily as in a sanctuary. If we prefer our harmless pleasures, we can justify them by asserting that God is as available on the golf course as at church (but how many golfers think of anything beyond the game they are in?).

There is only one valid excuse for maintaining a separation from the institutions of the Religions: the mature, thought-through conviction that one's personal beliefs disqualify him from any but a hypocritical affiliation. But then let this same high standard prevail in all that a person does, and let him demand a comparable perfection from his country club, his Rotary Club, from his professional society.

Hypocrisy comes from a Greek word which means acting, as in the theater. Hypocrisy is acting against what we actually believe. Surely it is unnecessary to say that it is sounder for a person to stay away from the Religions than to pretend falsely that he can be within. Yet there is nevertheless still another word

118

to be said: It is to ourselves that we need to be true; it is against ourselves that hypocrisy is a glaring offense.

More than once, when I attend worship, I am expected to read passages — usually ancient ones — which I simply do not believe. At times I simply abstain from reading such passages; at other times, I focus on what I sense is the intent in a passage, and though the words could possibly put me off, my grasp of the intent behind the words can satisfy me.

At stake is the issue: What do I personally want from public worship service? I think that what I want most is some mood that matches my bent. I can remember when words I could not believe in in a service put me off; I think this is no longer the case with me, for I have developed a certain toleration for the circumstance that no author, however skillful, can provide a prayerbook which will suit every single worshiper in every way. In return for the rather clear benefits to me from public worship, the conscious theological reservations I have about certain passages are of little consequence to me; since a public worship utilizes ancient materials, such reservations seem inevitable. I do not believe that Moses wrote the Pentateuch; a passage in a worship service which assumes or asserts that he did does not trouble me — though I would prefer that the passage weren't there. It would be hypocrisy only if outside the context of a worship service, such as a study group, I pretended to believe what I do not. As is true in other areas of life, religion has also devised a rhetoric of its own, and we err when we try to identify the ordinary rhetoric of religion with mature belief.

In all honesty, I am more distracted by such things as a preacher's wretched grammar or an ill-prepared sermon than by the infelicities of the prayerbook. The music can distract me, for often able singers present fourth-rate compositions or unable singers torture first-rate music, to the point that I yearn for their silence. Must they sing at me, not to me? And must people whisper so loud as to have me hear what is not intended for me? In sum, my dissatisfactions with the prayerbook are small compared with other recurring dissatisfactions.

119

I put my emphasis on the mood of a service rather than on its doctrinal aspect for an additional reason. The world of sports and of movies conditions us to be spectators, and often when we attend worship, it is as spectators, not as participants. Let it be granted that ofttimes the inherited forms of worship and deplorable procedures by the clergy tend to make a worship service an occasion for spectators. But the worshiper also has an obligation: to adjust himself into being a participant not merely an on-looker.

Finally, Is worship — public worship — an essential or only a frill? I find it hard to envisage religion without worship, though a silent prayer seems to me quite as worthy as the most approvable audible one. But public worship seems to me an essential ingredient to men, not only because we do not live solitary lives, but also because there can be palpable gains from it for him who participates. The danger that public worship will be mechanical, routine, or mere ostentation always lurks. But is not this regrettable risk found in all public endeavors?

All institutions, government, schools, and religions are susceptible of corruptions or of total corruption. These are forefended against from the inside, not the outside. The correction of abuse comes more strongly from within.

We can be bored at worship, despite our wish and intention not to be. But does modern man need to be as severe and hostile to public worship as now? I fear that some intolerance prevails.

If there are values we cherish, where and how are these preserved, perpetuated, and transmitted? By government? By schools? By institutional religion?

Is not the answer obvious?

XVIII

Prayer, Symbol, Ritual

WHAT MODERN MEN want to know are things like these:
Does God "hear" prayer? Does he "answer" prayer, responding to the person who is praying by giving what is asked for? If he does, prayer is surely worthwhile; if he does not, then what good is it?

In the past, and even in the present, the Religions have commonly assured ordinary people that prayers are ordinarily answered. The best minds in Religion have seen a double danger in such assurance. One danger is that men, on observing that prayers have often gone unanswered, come to feel that prayer is futile. A second danger is that of unreality, or of philosophical shallowness, and, indeed, prayer can as readily entail superstition as worship.

There are types of prayer which to good minds are frivolous. To pray for a new dress, or for the rain to stop so a picnic can be held as scheduled, is frivolous. Moreover, if a father is hard pressed financially and prays that his daughter not pray for a new dress, at the same moment that she prays for it, whom is God to please? If a farmer needs rain when the picnicker wants a clear day, whose prayer is to prevail? Again, if God is capable of being influenced by prayer, is not the prayer at the moment more powerful than God? (Medieval scholastics considered this latter a very important item.) Indeed, if praying is deemed to be coercing God, then such unconscious coercion is really superstition. A prayer which asks for something is called *petitionary*.

But a prayer need not ask for something specific such as a

121

dress or a clear day. In fact, it might not ask for anything at all, but simply reflect the mood of a worshiper, a mood of exaltation and gratitude, or one of sorrow and discouragement. Nonpetitionary prayer has something of a similarity to a completely human situation in which one person feels the need to speak to some other person whose wisdom he trusts — not to receive guidance or approval but simply to have a "sounding board" to help him clarify his own confusions or work out of his array of distresses. Prayer of this kind is, of course, far different from the frivolity of silly requests.

Indeed, we all face recurrent situations, or indeed crises, in which a sense of direction eludes us, or an ability to weigh intangible factors is beyond us, or a calamity (such as the serious illness of a loved one) hangs over us, or disaster strikes us. Often it is some kind of deep desperation, some intolerable anxiety, that moves us to pray. In such situations, the question of whether or not some divine intervention, some miracle, will ensue is indeed present, but is quite secondary to the human need to articulate one's profound emotions. In a way, such situations reflect basic instincts. If our canoe tips over, we may shout, "Help!" We might be appealing to God; we might only be calling to friends who are close by. The calm question of whether God or some friend will hear our call for help is remote from the spontaneity with which we can shout, "Help!" There are those who speak on behalf of prayer by suggesting that the act of praying is a boon to the person praying. Obviously this is the case, for just as some of us can gain relief in losing our tempers or in giving way to merited tears, so the cry to God for help can assuage the person who so cries.

Yet such an endorsement of prayer, perceptive and affirmative as it is, runs a risk of distorting the meaning, for if a prayer can only give psychological help to the person praying, it scarcely conforms to a proper definition of prayer, speech addressed to God. It may well be, as I personally believe, an adequate justification for praying, but one ought to recognize that this understanding of prayer can be a subterfuge for evading the need to answer the questions, Does God hear prayers, and Does he answer them? If we grant that frivolous prayers are unworthy of any consideration by mature people, then, respecting non-petitionary prayers*, one enters into the area of what one believes, not what one knows.

Should one pray? Obviously one should, provided only that one finds value for oneself in it. The acute problem, so it seems to me, is that most of us assume that because we must reject frivolous petitionary prayer, we become hypocrites if we pray in any way at all. Out of our wish to avoid hypocrisy, we tend to develop a total reluctance, a total indisposition, to prayer.

What can one do when one finds some inner block to an instinctive human impulse to pray? Perhaps one can come to cultivate the disposition. One might, for example, pray silently. Or, one might use a traditional prayerbook, if its use helps one out of one's inability to fashion the requisite words. Let one then use a prayerbook, not in the literal sense of the prayers, but in terms of one's own convictions and understanding. Let no one be ashamed whether his disposition is to pray or not to. Let one be honest with one's self.

What praying achieves, at least in my view, is to help one reach out beyond the world of mundane affairs, to attune oneself to what is deeper and greater than man. I do not place great importance on the particular words spoken, if any; I do see significance in prayer as a reflection of man's comprehension of his transcient role in a mysterious world. To stifle an impulse to prayer on philosophical or theological grounds seems to me to be unhuman.

Surely, one should not trivialize prayer. I know of few things I regard as silly, and even as abominable, as the American custom of invocations and benedictions by clergymen at meetings

---

*At dinner at my home, one of my sons asked our visitor, a Catholic priest, why a certain basketball player crossed himself before trying to shoot a foul. I was quickly fearful that my teenager had offended our guest. The priest replied, without a second's hesitation, "Superstition."

123

of social workers, philanthropic fund-raising affairs, or college football games in the southern states.

I think it well to train children to pray, but I think it is abominable to force them to. Regular prayer at meal-times in a family ought to cease when the merest suspicion arises that the children find it tedious, useless, or empty. If prayer does not come from the willing heart, it is better for it to be skipped than to be superimposed. Children can be forced to pray; they cannot be forced to want to pray.

A symbol is a tangible sign which visually represents what could otherwise require endless words. An American flag epitomizes our Declaration of Independence and our Constitution; as the epitome of these tremendously important legacies, the flag is more than just the cloth from which it is made. There is always the danger of patrioteering, of distorting patriotism into cheap and tawdry political devices. No greater distortion is possible, though, than of making a symbol an end in itself, rather than using its proper function as a representation of something fuller and deeper.

Religious symbols — such as the Cross or the Star of David — can also properly epitomize visually the historic significance of a tradition, or in religious patrioteering, they can become something merely magical.

The issue is not about a symbol itself, but the use to which we put a symbol.

By and large, a symbol is something static. A religious ritual is a symbol that is acted out.

Religious rituals ought never be confused with magic. In my experience and observation, they enrich a home. What is gained from them is well worth the effort.

We humans are so constituted that in many a situation, a symbol, when we understand it, can have a beauty and an impact that is denied even the most eloquent words.

There are those good people, usually older ones, whose negative attitude to symbol or ritual is conveyed in a sentence, once frequent but today curiously less so: "My religion is the Golden

Rule. I need no rituals." Would that all people and all nations did live the Golden Rule!

But the full range of human experience goes beyond even the highest of ethical injunctions, for the milestones of birth and death are inescapable realities not truly touched by ethics alone. Moreover, the Golden Rule (Leviticus 19:18; Mark 12:31) can be at most a general statement; it can fall short of enlightening us in the stance we are compelled to assume respecting the complexities of the intertwining of economics and ethics in our highly industrialized world.

No one in his right mind is against the Golden Rule. Yet it is susceptible to being used merely as a slogan, and a superficial one at that; it is too simple a stance to be able to meet the acute problems of living. A personal dedication to a worthy ethical precept is insufficient for all the nuances that living engenders. My own observation is that those who regard the Golden Rule as religion enough have been turned off by previous exposure to empty rituals or have been mistakenly led at some time to equate religious rituals with superstition. Yet even if this latter is not the case, and a person, supposedly thinking things through, concludes that ritual is not right for him, then well and good — for him.

But symbols and rituals are inherent human predilections. We express our patriotism not by reciting the Preamble to the Constitution but by our respect for the flag of our country. An engagement ring is only a rounded piece of metal, possibly with one or more precious stones, but for a man to give it to a woman entails more than the transfer of some metal and stones, and in those sad cases where an engagement is broken and the ring returned, more is at stake than the valuable trinket, since hopes, affections, confidences, plans, and expectations are all overtones of the giving of the ring, and its return is their bitter frustration.

It is futile to commend a reasonable attitude towards ritual to the person whose disposition makes him averse to it. For those who are not afflicted by a blind hostility towards ritual, it is perhaps possible to say, "Many religious rituals began as superstitions. The supersititious aspects can be winnowed away, and a worthy, beautiful, and significant residue remain."

Symbol and ritual should serve us; ritual becomes a distortion if it is supposed that we must serve it. All too often the Religions have assumed that they exist to be served and, indeed, for men to be enslaved to them. No, the Religions exist to serve men, not men the Religions.

Symbol and ritual can enhance that part of our nature that bends towards, and responds, to beauty, and that is why so many artisans have fashioned wondrous examples of religious symbol and ritual objects.

In the same way that a flag can express and stir our patriotism, so a religious ritual can be a completely human, highly esthetic way of deepening whatever measure of religious fervor we begin with. It is not the abstractions of the Constitution, or the abstractions of a Religion, that tug us and draw us along; rather, symbol and ritual do this in ways that words alone seldom can.

XIX

Fate and Free Will

DO WE DO what we do because we are controlled by some force (shall we call it fate?) which preordains our actions? Or do we do what we do as a result of our own free choice? When things happen to us, things in which we have had no opportunity to choose, has it been because of fate or has it been sheer accident? Few abstract problems in the history of man's thought are more ancient, and only the problem of evil seems to have oppressed man more than this question about *fate* and *free will*. Pagan religion, in at least two forms which we will look at, was permeated by such problems; they have inevitably entered into Judaism and Christianity.

If we are to understand fate in the pagan sense, we need some definitions or, rather, distinctions. Fate as a force is not the same as simple cause and effect. When the brakes of a car are faulty and this occasions a collision, that is a matter of cause and effect. The explanation offered for the weakness of the brakes also deals with cause and effect, as, for example, when the requisite brake fluid has drained out and the brakes did not hold out. The area of fate is different. If we say that some unseen force ordained that the brake fluid leak out, that the car should be driven to a certain place by a certain route, and that the car to be collided with should be at the given place at the given time, then this would all be fate. If we call the collision an accident, we are using a word which is the exact opposite of fate; *fate* implies a force which ordains what takes place, while *accident* implies that no ordaining force was operating.

127

The word *fate* comes from the Latin *fatum*, "what has been spoken," this in the sense of something already decreed. Among the Greeks, fate was called in early times *ātē* (or *moira*, or the "Errynes"), and in later times *heimarmene*. Within this development, three sisters often symbolized aspects of fate: Clotho, who spun the thread of a man's life; Lachesis, who twisted the thread; and, Atropos who with a scissors cut it off to end it. The roles of the sisters covered the totality of a man's life.

The Greek gods were also deemed subject to fate.

The tragedy of man lay in his powerlessness to escape from the decrees of blind fate. The story of Oedipus is not, as it has been since its use in Freudian psychology, the matter of a son's eroticism towards his mother, but rather the account of how futile and tragic is was for Oedipus to try to escape the fate decreed for him, namely, to do the abominable — killing his father and marrying his mother. In the play of Sophocles, Oedipus is told of his fate and flees in attempt to escape it, but, unaware, he does exactly what he fled to avoid. He could not escape his fate.

To some Greeks, the idea that fate so controlled events as to deprive man of any capacity for choice of any kind was offensive. A kind of compromise idea was at times proposed which, without denying fate, left some room for a person to make some choices.*

It is a universal experience of man that some events seem very much the opposite of accident; hence, some idea about fate, expressed in varying forms, is found in almost every civilization, whether among the Norse or the ancient Babylonians. The latter, for example, ascribed the power of fate to the stars, and even taught that man could discover what his fate would be by "reading" the stars. The latter "science" is called astrology; the astrologer was a usual character in any sumptuous court, even in late medieval times, and astrology columns appear in many

*In some dictionaries and encyclopedias, this middle view goes under the name *determinism*; one should be warned that in others, determinism is defined as if it is interchangeable with fate.

contemporary newspapers. Philo of Alexandria, whom we have already mentioned, believed that the future could indeed be read in the stars; however, in his view it was blasphemy to believe that the stars controlled the future, for that belief ascribed to created things the power that could belong only to the creator.

What is at stake if one believes that a power — fate — exists and that one cannot escape from this power? In answer, the implication is that our lives are only an acting out of what has already been decided about us and for us. We can do nothing at all to escape our fate; if we are poor and hungry and oppressed, we are powerless to seek any relief or remedy, for the decrees of fate are not subject to change. People speak of inexorable fate; *inexorable* means "incapable of being prayed to"; one cannot pray to fate for its decrees to be changed. Hence, for the suffering person — and at some point all people suffer — there is no way out of that which is supposedly decreed for one. Hence, man is alone in a cold and unfriendly universe — the kind of "absurd" world that the nonreligious existentialists of recent decades have spoken about in essays, novels, and plays.

In the Hebrew Bible, as we have said, the view is that God controls history. In a sense, this view is somewhat kindred to fate, but it has two striking differences. One difference is that it is never assumed that a person is without some capacity to choose. Rather, a person can choose, and he bears responsibility for the choice which he has made. Second, God, unlike fate, can be appealed to — prayed to — and therefore man's destiny is not fixed and immutable. Moreover, while fate is a force unconcerned about what happens to nations and men, God is depicted as very much concerned. Indeed, he is viewed as "watching over" men in order to avert danger, should it arise, or to intervene and rescue a nation or a man from a threatening danger. The term ordinarily used is *God's providence*, "God's watchful, protective concern."

The contrast could scarcely be sharper than between man's helplessness and loneliness in a hostile world ruled by fate and his sense of having God as a companion and guide who is able to protect and guide him in a world beneficently ruled. It is this latter which is the theme of the best known of all the Psalms, the Twenty-third:

> God is my shepherd, I do not lack,
> He leads me beside still waters; he
>   brings me back. . .
> Even though I walk in the darkest of
>   valleys, I do not fear evil,
> For Your [God's] rod and staff comfort me.

It is conceivable that the spread of Judaism and, later, that of Christianity into the Grecian world was the result of this message of God's loving guidance, for it offered to men a solace that was in marked contrast to the impersonality of a cruel world dominated by an unchangeable fate.

The Jewish-Christian belief in providence, like all beliefs, was susceptible of distortion. In one direction, it could lead, as it did, to a use of amulets (the tacit purpose of which was to coerce God) or to lead the foolhardy into risks and dangers from which only miraculous divine intervention could save them. (This is the attitude criticized in the phrase "to tempt providence.") In another distortion, there have been those who, occupying a gratifying status in society, have felt the conviction that God had ordained them for such a gratifying role; this is the bare meaning of the term *predestination*. It has been all too easy for a person to assert his special privilege of power, wealth, nobility, or royalty by ascribing it to predestination, that is, God had picked out some fortunate man for his high estate and the poor and hungry for their low estate.

In Paul's scheme of things, for example, man was viewed as lacking the choice to do something, and also the ability of doing anything successfully. Paul taught that one could not truly successfully observe the Jewish laws, and hence man could not "earn" redemption. To whom then did redemption come? Paul's answer was that it came to those whom God predestined for it.

130

In a sense, predestination can differ very little from the Greek view of fate, the difference being whether the destiny originates from a blind force, as in Greek paganism, or from God, as in Judaism and Christianity.

A dilemma that can arise for men is the following: If one emphasizes predestination, the inference would be that man is no more than a puppet and without social responsibility or occasion for ethical choice. On the other hand, to emphasize man's full freedom to choose can imply that God's providence is so unimportant that it does not truly exist. To hold to predestination and to deny free will, or vice versa, is to run counter to much of the remaining substance of the Religions. If man is without choice and only acting out what is foreordained for him, it is futile to exhort him, in Sabbath services, to ethical conduct; on the other hand, if there is no guiding divine providence, man is in as lonely and hopeless a situation as if he were guided by blind fate.

There is no philosophic solution for this dilemma of fate and free will. The Religions advocate a harmonization of the conflicting views, usually tacitly, as if to imply that one should hold on to both beliefs without carrying them to the extremes wherein the one belief negates the other. An ancient rabbi "solved" the dilemma by asserting that both determinism and free will existed.

Because the doctrines predestination and free will are beliefs, and therefore beyond man's knowledge, modern man has usually been unconcerned with them. If anything, modern man was impelled by the Renaissance and subsequent humanism man was impelled by the Renaissance and subsequent humanism to stress, as if against Paul, man's possession of the capacity yo progress towards an ever greater future. The poem *Invictus* by William Ernest Henley (1848-1903) begins:

> Out of the night that covers me,
>   Black as the pit from pole to pole
> I thank whatever gods may be
>   For my inconquerable soul.

It ends with these two lines:

> I am the master of my fate;
> I am the captain of my soul.

In our time, surely the boast of being "the master of my fate" is an obscenity. Let one only inquire of those who survived the Nazi conquests of their lands whether they can accept this sentiment.

One need not necessarily believe in the ancient Greek notion of a blind, inexorable fate, and that man is totally helpless, and totally without capacities. One can be uneasy about man's capacities without ascribing none at all to him.

The basic issue in our perilous times, in view of the very recency of worldwide upheavals, is between those who embrace the view that all is absurd and futile and those who yearn to find some meaning in life — to discover for themselves some sense of personal significance in their having lived.

Possibly the view that life is absurd is right. But it passes my understanding how people can live by that view. If the alternative is only an illusion, or only a delusion, this choice, if one can hold it, is preferable to a commitment to ultimate futility.

XX

Jesus

THE PURPOSE of this chapter is to explain. It does not try to go beyond that.

First of all, Christ is not the last name of Jesus. It is something of a title, something of an effort to indicate the role Christendom ascribes to him. The word is Greek; it is a translation of a Hebrew word *messiah*, whose meaning is "anointed with oil." Among the Hebrews such anointment was a symbol; in its earliest use, it was the ceremony by which a commoner was raised to royalty; in that sense, "the anointed one" was another way of saying, "the acknowledged king." In the Hebrew Bible, the anointing of a legitimate king, such as Saul or David, was done by a prophet, Samuel; this at the behest of God. Therefore, the person anointed had his legitimacy asserted or justified by divine sanction.

When the Babylonians conquered Judea in 587 B.C., they sent into exile the last of the kings of the dynasty of David, and when this king (Jehoiachin) died, kingship terminated, and for almost four centuries the Hebrews were without a king. In exile in Babylon, they yearned to return to Judea; they yearned for self-government there, under a Judean king. This latter yearning they expressed in their hopes and prayer that God would send them a "Messiah."

With the passing of more time, the word gained additional overtones. When the Persians conquered the Babylonians, they allowed the Judeans to return home, to be ruled by a Persian governor and a Jewish high priest, not a king. In turn, the

133

Greeks, under Alexander the Great of Macedonia, supplanted the Persians, and, after Alexander's death, Judea fell to one of his generals, Seleucus, whose kingdom was centered in Antioch in Syria. Not only were the Judeans without their king and a subject people, but they suffered from the warfares with and the hostility from the surrounding peoples. They couched their wish for relief by the prayer that God should alter their miserable situation for the better by sending the Messiah.

Moreover, the ancient prophets had spoken of the great glories of the remote future, when, at the end of time, God would redress all the injustices that had existed by bringing his final judgment onto the world. There were those who felt that the Messiah, so long yearned for, would come only at the time of the last judgment. Also, Jews had scattered throughout the civilized world, from where, according to ancient prophecy, they would some day be miraculously gathered and restored to Judea. That event, too, came to be bound up with the future advent of the Messiah. Later many, perhaps most, Jews began to believe in resurrection; there were those who extended the future judgment over nations into a judgment over individual men. That remote future moment of individual judgment was viewed as destined to arrive only when the Messiah would come.

Judea gained independence from the Seleucidians after their revolt in 168 B.C. The leading family, the Maccabeans, founded a new dynasty about 150 B.C. which received the support of recognition by Rome, which had come to exert its power in the eastern Mediterranean. But the dynasty did not last, for Rome conquered Judea in 63 B.C.; in 37, a non-Maccabean, Herod the Great, came to the throne as a "client king," that is, a subject of Rome; he reigned until his death in 4 B.C., the year when, according to some Christian reckoning, Jesus was born. Before the time of Jesus, oppression by Herod or the Romans led to outbreaks here and there of guerilla warfare. In such disorders and sufferings, relief was prayed for, again in terms of the Messiah, but with the hope that he would come soon, not in the remote future. Since the latter Maccabeans were scarcely worthy men, and Herod a man of unique cruelty (and ability), a proper Jewish king could be neither a Maccabean nor a Herodian, but, hopefully, a descendant of David.

In Jewish terms, the Messiah would be a man sent by God; he would be a descendant of David. He would terminate Rome's hold over the land, and himself rule over his people. At this advent, the great judgment day — over men and nations — would come; the sufferings of the Judeans would be changed into joy and triumph, the Judeans scattered throughout the world miraculously returned to Judea, and the resurrection time would arrive.

Jesus was regarded, at least by his followers, fellow Jews, as the long awaited Messiah who had come at last to usher in the tremendous events of judgment day.

He died by crucifixion (about A.D. 30, at a juncture when a series of Roman "procurators" had come to rule in place of Herod's son Archelaus, deposed in A.D. 6). His followers believed he had been granted a special resurrection in advance of the general resurrection expected to come some day. He had ascended to heaven, but would soon return to usher in the judgment day. We should here notice that the ordinary Jewish expectation was that the Messiah, in a single advent, would usher in the great events, and that Christians conceived instead of two steps, the initial appearance that had already taken place, and the "second coming," hoped for in the near future.

The new movement, spurred by the belief in the resurrection of Jesus, grew and spread. In the Greek world it attracted Gentiles. A translation of the beliefs and the ideas of the new movement took place; the title *Messiah* was translated as "Christ." Just as we would say Doctor Jones, or Smith, the Professor, so Greek Gentile Christians spoke either of Christ Jesus or Jesus Christ.

But a change even greater than mere translation was taking place. The role which Jews saw in the Messiah as the national, even military, rescuer of his people was decisively altered; the Christ came to be viewed as involved not in freeing Judeans

135

from Rome but in freeing mankind from its bondage to sin. The death of Jesus was regarded as the freeing, redemptive act.*

The Messiah, we have said, was deemed to have been sent by God. Christians, whether in Judea or later in the Greek world, regarded the word Christ as signifying the divine role of Jesus, holding that Jesus was not only sent by God, but was in some sense divine. *Christ* became the shortened way to express the special divinity of Jesus. Other terms were used: Son of David, Lord, Son of God. The preeminent word, though, was *Christ*.

The usual Christian view was this, that the divine Christ had come to earth, there to become the man Jesus. This Jesus had had an earthly career which included his death and resurrection, and, to repeat, had ascended to heaven to God to await the near moment of his return, his second coming.

The word Christ is an answer, so we may say, to the question of *what* was Jesus. The accounts of his birth, his career, his trial, his death tell *who* he was.

Four such accounts appear in the New Testament; each is called a Gospel, and specifies the author (all of whom are now considered unknown) by appending to the word Gospel the phrase, *According to Matthew*, or *According to Mark, to Luke*, or *to John*.

Modern Christian scholarship has some opinions that represent a rather broad consensus: First, the Gospels were written between forty and sixty years after the date of the death of Jesus.

---

*As is well known, traditional Jews still await the coming of the Messiah. Whatever may have been the achievements and high worth of Jesus, what Jews expected from the Messiah did not come from him. Ordinary Jews and Christians are unaware that the common word *Messiah* means totally different things to the two communities, and, naturally, do not grasp or agree with what the other community accepts. Jews do not attribute Messiahship or special divinity to Jesus. Moreover, the Messiah idea, central to Christianity, is hardly as central to Judaism, being more periphal in importance.

The paradox thus arises that Christians have an esteem for Jesus a Jew which Jews have lacked, and the communities in this matter are ordinarily remote from any common plane of possible genuine discourse.

Enough time had passed for convictions about "Christ" to become deepened and relatively stabilized; it is to be noted that the earliest Christian writings were the Epistles of Paul, replete with convictions about the Christ. Second, in the interval between the death of Jesus and the writing of the Gospels, theological convictions had developed further, and normal legends arose, and these are reflected within the Gospels. Third, the Gospel writers were not modern historians, but devout Christians, and their concern was not pure history as modern scholars understand history, but, instead, a mixture of reliable history and of didactic, theological and legendary materials.

Only in a general way, so the scholars say, can the historical facts about Jesus be established. There seems no reason, though, to doubt that he was a Galilean Jew whose home was Nazareth, that his career involved teaching and leadership, that the title Messiah was claimed for him, either by himself or his followers, or both. That he is a historical person seems to prudent students to offer no basis for doubt. That we cannot be precise about the historical data is also a fact. We cannot really know what kind of man he was.

The inquiry into what kind of a man Jesus was represents a significant reversal, already mentioned (page 100). The early church was persuaded of his divinity but was host to quarrels about his humanity. In the past two hundred years, many Christians, including dignitaries, have come to question, doubt, or reinterpret the belief in his divinity. A good many people, not believing literally in the divinity of Jesus, point (correctly) to his surpassing importance to the history of the world after his time, and they have sought for or devised a view which makes Jesus only human, but also a man whose nobility of character and purpose, and unique capacity to understand life and teach about it, establish him as a foremost man of all time, indeed, a person after whom modern people can model themselves.

The new view of Jesus lends itself to inspirational books. Such books are often the despair of the learned scholars; these ordinarily hold that insufficient secure data about Jesus are avail-

137

able for a biography to be written or for anything definite to be asserted. The scholars are, of course, right; but those who have written "inspirational," non-scholarly books have tried to meet the particular needs of men who require a credible Jesus-figure but who cannot accept the theological Jesus of Christian doctrine. Some of the inspirational books about Jesus are cheap and capricious; some are not. There is, however, seldom a real relationship between the Jesus of a modern "biographer," or a modern musical, and the Jesus presented in the Gospels.

Some general comments might be in order for those who wish something sounder than the inspirational books. Jesus was a Jew, not a Christian. He was central in early Christian faith, not because he was a great teacher (as he probably was) and not because he was a kindly man who went around loving people (this is fiction, not fact!), but because he was viewed as divine, a divine being who had become man, and through his death sinful mankind was redeemed. To make Jesus only a teacher, or only a social reformer, or only a religious reformer, as do such books (this latter is an untenable view), does considerable violence to the documents preserved by Christianity.

One more matter. The Christian tradition lauds the sacrificial death of Jesus and at the same time has blamed Jews — all Jews of all ages! — for being allegedly responsible for his death. The exact "facts" about his trial and execution cannot be recovered. It is strange, but human, that the Christians have viewed him as redeeming mankind from sin and of reconciling man to God, but until recent times have had no wish for reconciliation with Jews and little desire to balance a loving Jesus with some love for non-Christians and some charity towards Jews. Christianity has fostered and perpetuated anti-Semitism; Christian anti-Semitism made Hitler's anti-Semitism possible. Christianity has as yet far from purged itself completely of this disease, though many individual Christians have.

Naturally, loyal Christians relish the figure of a noble, kindly Jesus, the Christian of all Christians. It is understandable that they would prefer to have a Christian Jesus they can grasp and identify with than a Galilean Jew they can neither grasp nor identify with. There is much that is appealing in the ascriptions of nobility and kindliness to Jesus.

But perhaps one might wish for a bit more rigor and a little less sentimentality and superficiality. The New Testament view of the Christ — whether one accepts it or not — is a formidable, exciting challenge to a curious mind and heart.

There would seem today to be two different views of Jesus. One is an authentically Christian view, regarding him as a divine savior. There is another Jesus, a Jesus of modern culture; such a Jesus is quite different from the authentic Christian Jesus.

XXI

The Clergy

THE MINISTRY as a profession — that is, a means of earning a living — is a relatively new development, scarcely over a hundred years old. True, before then, Catholic and Anglican priests were supported financially by "benefits of the clergy," but that was much different from the modern arrangement, especially among Jews and Protestants, in which the clergyman receives a stipulated monthly or annual wage for his services to a local church. The earlier arrangement was for a man to earn his livelihood by a trade, and to serve his church on a voluntary basis.

That one should be paid to serve God is surely monstrous; Jews got around this valid objection by paying a rabbi what was called *sechar bittul*, compensation for "foregoing"; that is, he was paid not for his religious work, but in recognition that he could have earned his livelihood by some other means, and his pay is for what he does not earn by this other means! How often I have heard people speak of the best kind of a clergyman as a "spiritual" man, and how readily a clergyman can lose the reputation of being spiritual if he exhibits even the slightest interest in money — even if for food or his children's clothing or education.

In Protestantism, the clergy, especially in the non-ritual churches, were treated (and many still are) as wards of the charity of parishioners. We are not far removed in time from "poundings," a festivity to which church members brought a pound of this or a pound of that for the preacher. His children were usually picked out to receive the hand-me-downs of a family which ran out of its own children to give them to.

Now, it is to be lamented that society has so changed that the ministry has become a profession, but the fact is that it has. The minister may get a "clergy discount" here and there (at times in humiliating circumstances), but the reality is that he now pays for bread, gasoline, school books, and shoes exactly what everyone else pays. The railroads used to have "clergy" fares; most airlines do not. How, then, is a minister to feed, clothe, and provide a house or apartment for his family without somehow having some contact with greenbacks and metal coins?

On what scale shall he and his family live? Mere subsistence? Or better than mere subsistence? Should he live as well as a plumber, or a physician, or the owner of a lucrative factory? When is he "underpaid"?

What is reasonably to be expected of him?

"Let him be a spiritual man!" Of course! That means that he must possess an array of human virtues: mental alertness, a decent schooling, a good ability at public speaking, the wisdom to be a responsible counsellor, dignity and warmth in marrying and burying, and some capacity to "get along with people." Our society makes Willy Lomans ("They like me!") out of the clergy more thoroughly than out of all other classes of men.

Not only must he possess the human virtues, but he must be free of human frailties. He must not forget appointments, never let himself be irked, never be bored, never feel put upon, never lose his temper, smile in all personal adversity, and deprive himself of every shred of family privacy. Let him have some frailties, and he ceases "to be liked," he ceases to be "spiritual."

But, more profoundly, his role — in Protestantism or Judaism, and more recently even to some extent in Catholicism — as a professional person leads to a genuine and serious tension. Is the minister of a church, or a rabbi, the employee of his retainers and subject to their will and whims, or is he their leader, and are his retainers his followers? Modern religious organizations have never solved this basic problem, simply because it is beyond solution. The clergy and his retainers can often find a modus vivendi in favorable circumstances. But latent is a tension that periodically comes to the fore. Has a clergyman the personal right to march to Selma, speak out against inadequate housing in his community, and picket the White House over Viet Nam? Or does he need the prior approval of his retainers and must he obey their mandates? What price must he be made to pay for those stands on principle that his reatiners view as indiscrete, irrelevant, unwise, or simply wrong? Or, from the other side, must a Catholic parishioner in the fruit business continue his generous support of a church whose rector publicly urges a boycott of grapes or lettuce? Do external circumstances impel parishioners to want to limit the ordinary freedom of the clergyman? Should the clergyman pusillanimously capitulate? Should he jeopardize his job (and salary) and the means by which, if married and a parent, he supports his family?

I think that it is relatively seldom that a direct tension between a clergyman and his congregation comes to the surface. I think that there is very often a lurking tension that manages not to come to the surface. My acquaintance with clergy leads me to believe that the lurking tension is more debilitating to them than the overt.

I know of no other profession in which the trespass of the one is used to indict all. Surely, since clergymen are human, individuals will do unseemly things: lying, stealing, or having sexual affairs. One would scarcely know from the estimate which the public holds of the clergy that overwhelmingly they are decent, honorable, hard-working men. In modern literature they are normally portrayed as the hypocritical bigot in Maugham's *Rain*, or the doddering idiot in *Life With Father*. In movies, the Catholic priest is usually an affirmative character, especially in older Bing Crosby films, with a masculinity that supposedly underlines his celibacy, but the worst "pornography" I can recall in recent times has been novels about priests. Among Jews, there is a joke in which a father, bragging about his sons, says, "My oldest is a doctor, my second a lawyer, and my third

142

— ah, he's a rabbi, and what kind of job is that for a Jewish boy?"

The reality is that modern society, eternally confusing superstition and religion, wants the clergyman to be a worker of magic, not a rational, self-respecting man.

No one, so I can boast, knows more than I do about unseemly aspects of the deeds and lives of some clergymen, or is more cognizant of widespread shortcomings such as the intellectual inadequacy, the poverty in insight and comprehension of many, and a needless sense of insecurity. Nevertheless, I can say in truth that our age has a remarkably gifted clergy of dedicated and decent men.

Not one of them is superhuman. Not one is free of some personal frailty. But still, as a class, they are a superb group of human beings.

What should we want from a clergyman? First of all, personal integrity and probity. Second, he ought to be an effective person (that is, neither a misfit nor lamentably stupid). Third, he ought to be responsive to human needs. Fourth, he ought to be well-schooled and tolerably wise. Last of all, he ought to be good at preaching* and the other routine chores that fall on him.

---

*Historically the sermon began as an explanation of Scripture. That was the case in the early synagogue which was a unique institution in that it was something of a school and quite distinct from the Temple in Jerusalem, where animal sacrifices were offered. *Synagogue* is a Greek word meaning "the act of assembly" or "place of assembly"; the term synagogue is Jewish by association, not etymology. When Jews gathered for instruction in Scripture, they took the first step in fashioning this form of teaching. Gradually prayer accompanied the study, and the synagogue became a place of worship as well as a school. A local church is a Christian form of a synagogue, being directly derived. As ritual increased and fixed, prayer grew, the sermon receded in importance, virtually disappearing in Catholicism and traditional Judaism. It was revived to a central place in worship in Protestantism and liberal Judaism.

American synagogues are often called *temples*, especially by Reform Jews. Such temples, though, are synagogues, not temples.

143

What ought society do about the clergy? First and foremost, to free them of routine financial worries so that they can carry out their duties, not worry about food for their children. To provide them with some facilities — not necessarily a luxurious sanctuary — and some secretarial help so that they do not become secretaries. Next, provide them with adequate pension and retirement benefits so that they do not serve in old age simply to continue to earn a living. And next, abstain from treating them in a paternalistic, humiliating way (such as underpaying them in salary and then giving them gifts they may or may not want).

But most of all, let society regard them as assets. Only the misfit among the clergy could not have bettered themselves financially if they had chosen some other profession. Let the clergy, then, pursue their difficult, trying profession with all the dignity and devotion that most have shown they can muster.

XXII

On Being Religious

WE HAVE TRAVERSED, however briefly, a very great deal, perhaps so much that, understandably, a reader here or there may feel overwhelmed. I hope this is not the case.

Let me here try to draw together those threads that have seemed to me the most important.

I have stressed the personal — the individual — as paramount over the institutional; I have, though, indicated the possible worthy role of the institutions. I have tried to clarify belief as distinct from knowledge and to show what is at stake in beliefs. I have abstained from saying everything I could say, even in subjects where I could say a great deal more, in the hope that I have been able to point towards a breadth of understanding, not full depth. I have wanted, above all, to have the reader feel that there is some validity in religion and in the Religions.

Granted that on occasion we face crises which call for split-second decisions; that is not the case with what we have discussed in this book. In the realm of religion, the beliefs we come to hold have no need to arise as split-second conclusions. Indeed, the issues need not obsess us by becoming conscious preoccupations. Rather, it is better for them to be part of our latent awareness, and for them to grow and mature within us over a period of months or even years as we recur to this item or that item from time to time.

There are academic disciplines in the field of religion: Bible, medieval philosophy, social ethics, and the like. I have not supposed, and do not suppose, that the reader must be an academician in religion. No, let the reader know enough, and tolerably accurately, so that he or she has a sense of understanding.

If he understands, then let him take subsequent steps in accordance with his personal bent. I have from time to time likened religion to the arts, to music, to literature, in the sense that these enrich life. If our lives are bare of these, we are scarcely more than animals.

Our personal religion (and what we do with it) is in a sense kindred to what we do with the arts. Religion, so I believe, goes beyond these in its significance, and in its capacity to enrich us. It can help us to profundity, it can move us toward self-understanding, it can give us a sense of our human dignity and worth. It can, without falsity, give us an achieved inner security — not a cheap "peace of mind" — and an inner strength that are the results only of understanding, honesty, and earnest probing.

If there is in us something that enables us to respond to religion, let us not withhold ourselves from so responding. And as we can grow in our knowledge of music and our response to it, so too can we grow in our inner religious depth.

It is ourselves, not others, we need to satisfy. Such satisfaction is attainable.

It is, like true virtue, its own reward.